Pas de Deux

Pas de Deux

Great Partnerships in Dance

Sarah Montague

Universe Books
New York

Dedication
To Mary Clarke and Clement Crisp

Published in the United States of America in 1981
by Universe Books
381 Park Avenue South, New York, N.Y. 10016
© 1981 by Universe Books

81 82 83 84 85/10 9 8 7 6 5 4 3 2 1

Printed in the United States of America

Library of Congress Cataloging in Publication Data

Montague, Sarah, 1955–
  Pas de deux.

  Includes index.
  1. Ballet dancing—Pas de deux. I. Title.
GV1788.2.P37M66   792.8′2   80-54502
ISBN 0-87663-346-7   AACR2
ISBN 0-87663-553-2 (pbk.)

Contents

Carlotta Grisi and Jules Perrot in *Giselle*

Introduction

Great partnerships, from Adam and Eve to Fred and Ginger, are compellingly magical. In love, we wonder what it is between two people that makes them think and feel alike. In dance, we have some of our most profoundly beautiful images, both abstract and dramatic, of communion on many levels. "There is a special magic," wrote Clive Barnes, "a certain one and one miraculously adding to make three, a process that makes the partnership somehow greater than the contributions of the pair as individuals." In the twentieth century, classical ballet has blossomed as never before, and with it, some of the most extraordinary performance relationships the world has ever seen.

Of course, in the purely literal sense, partners have existed ever since there has been dancing—and for ballet, since the late seventeenth century, when the art was codified

in France and women first began to dance professionally. But it was the Romantic movement in ballet, which had its official beginning in Marie Taglioni's performance in *La Sylphide* in 1832, that really began to charge the pas de deux with emotional meaning. Of the great Romantic ballerinas, several had very successful working partnerships: Taglioni, and later Carlotta Grisi, with the gifted dancer and choreographer Jules Perrot, and Fanny Cerrito with her husband Arthur Saint-Léon. One contemporary reviewer of Taglioni and Perrot in *La Sylphide* wrote, "They fully correspond to each other . . . it looked as though one breath swayed them, as though in a single gust, in one rush, they soared into the air." Much the same terms are often used today to try to express the mysterious way partners have of not only moving together, but of seeming to originate from the same source, creating the same atmosphere. "Ballet partnering . . . demands the utmost in physically intricate and emotionally evocative teamwork," wrote Tobi Tobias.

During the late nineteenth century, the art of

ballet dwindled, in many places, to a tawdry spectacle, and the role of the man, particularly, was reduced from partner to porter. It wasn't until the advent of Vaslav Nijinsky, near the beginning of this century, that the *danseur* began literally to leap back into prominence, and with him the importance of the rapport between men and women on the stage. Nijinsky with Tamara Karsavina and Mikhail Mordkin with Anna Pavlova were our first great twentieth-century partnerships.

Dancers and critics both have written about the elements that make a partnership work, and though they say different things about friendship, chemistry, and physical rapport, all agree that the rapport goes beyond the mere logistics of double work. That, as Karsavina wrote in the *Dancing Times,* "can be arrived at through practice and technical knowledge, but a fusion happens only on a spiritual level—a mutual inspiration." Cynthia Gregory says, "Partnering is a kind of friendship. Dancers have to respect each other, they have to really *see* each other, as persons as well as 'characters.'" And Lincoln Kirstein, in his *Ballet Alphabet,* has this memorable description: "Dancers who, from habit or preference, have frequently danced together, come to have a sense of each other's physical presence, which, translated into terms of dancing, is revealed to an audience as an exquisite mutual awareness or superhuman courtesy."

Oddly enough, some of our greatest models for the perfect dance pairing come from outside the world of ballet. There were Vernon and Irene Castle and, most of all, the team of Fred Astaire and Ginger Rogers. In *The Fred Astaire and Ginger Rogers Book,* Arlene Croce describes their effect. "He is his own form of theatre and we ask nothing more. But when he dances with Ginger we suddenly realize what further revelations that theatre can produce: it can encompass the principle of complementarity." Astaire and Rogers, as Melissa Hayden says, "presented to the audiences a complete relationship."

This is precisely what the best ballet partners do—present more fully the relationship depicted by the choreographer, in some cases adding an extra dimension by their own electricity. One of the most obvious and moving relationships is, of course, love. In his book *The Ballerina,* Richard Austin writes, "I know of no more exact representation of human love than the formal *pas de deux* of classical ballet. It is a kind of ritual; it follows a set pattern—the duet, the two variations and the coda; and it is built upon a rising emotional tension, all the more powerful because this is expressed with such calm deliberation." Or, as Barnes put it, "The classic adagio can either be a love duet or merely an act between

Fanny Cerrito and Arthur Saint-Léon

Vernon and Irene Castle. Photo: Museum of Modern Art/Film Stills Archive

Fred Astaire and Ginger Rogers in *Top Hat*. Photo: Museum of Modern Art/Film Stills Archive

consenting adults. When it is a love duet, it is so beautifully expressive—whether it is used dramatically by a choreographer, or is a formal classic pas de deux. A man and a woman, love and poetry." No one who saw Markova and Dolin in *Giselle* or Fonteyn and Nureyev in *Romeo and Juliet* will forget those lessons in love. On the other hand, George Balanchine's plotless ballets are open to numerous interpretations. Suzanne Farrell and Peter Martins in *Apollo* or *Chaconne* are telling us as much about the relation between god and man, and man and art, as about love. The dancers can mean anything and everything.

Despite this book, ballet partnerships are a rare conjunction of the stars in their heavens. Many of our greatest dancers, like Cynthia Gregory and Natalia Makarova, have never really had partnerships (though Makarova is forming one with Anthony Dowell), and for every marriage made in heaven, there are

many more made on earth, with feet of clay. Erik Bruhn, who had an extraordinary rapport with Carla Fracci, had an earlier and less successful partnership with Nora Kaye, who once propelled him into the wings during the "Black Swan" pas de deux. Kaye, a powerful and moving dramatic dancer, could be alarmingly robust on the stage. She had an even more disastrous encounter with Igor Youskevitch (who found the perfect complement in Alicia Alonso) when she knocked him out in Valerie Bettis's *A Streetcar Named Desire* and had to finish the famous rape scene alone. More faux pas than pas de deux.

But, miraculously, a handful of times, dancers have found the perfect stage rapport, when two move as one—ballets la belle, la perfectly swell romance. They were remarkably lucky—and so are we.

Anna Pavlova & Mikhail Mordkin

Some partnerships are as important for what they did as for what they were. Anna Pavlova and Mikhail Mordkin danced together for a very short time, but the excitement they generated on their triumphant tours blazed a trail for the legions of famous dancers who followed them. When Pavlova and Mordkin burst upon the scene, ballet in most countries had become, if it was known at all, lumbering, rococo, and sensationalist. "Then," as one writer noted, "when the hopes of lovers of dancing were lowest, Pavlova and Mordkin came to rekindle the desire for true poetry of motion."

Pavlova was a graduate of the Imperial Ballet School in St. Petersburg, while Mordkin was from the Bolshoi Theater in Moscow, but, even growing up apart, the two future partners had developed similar attitudes about the developments in dancing at that time. Mordkin was depressed by the archaic rigidity of Russian ballet after the turn of the century and chafed in secret against the endless formal restrictions surrounding productions and performances. Meanwhile, in St. Petersburg, Pavlova had already begun to work with Michel Fokine, the revolutionary choreographer who changed the look of ballet with his less structured approach to dance, which relied more on natural movement and less on the rigidly formal and outlandish productions made popular by Marius Petipa.

The two dancers were attracting attention in their separate worlds. After Pavlova's first appearance in Petipa's *The Vestal Virgin,* critic Valerian Svetloff rhapsodized: "She was delicate, svelte, and pliant like a reed, with the open expression of a little Spanish girl; ethereal and fleeting. She was as graceful and as

Duration of partnership: 1909–11
Companies: Diaghilev Ballets Russes, 1909; with members of the St. Petersburg and Moscow Imperial Ballets, and Anna Pavlova's company, 1910–11
Principal Ballets: *The Autumn Bacchanale, Coppélia, Giselle, The Legend of Azyiade, Egyptian Nights, Raymonda, Valse Caprice*

"In the dance they seemed indissoluble, the vital beauty of an Olympic victor and the delicacy and spells of eternal woman."

—Katherine Rose Bowditch

fragile as a piece of Sèvres porcelain." Fokine spoke of her as the perfect collaborator. In Moscow, Mordkin was gaining a reputation as a bold dancer and strong partner. As with the favorite children of equally prominent families, there was talk of a partnership for these two promising dancers, who had heard of each other but never met. Finally Pavlova did travel to Moscow to dance *La Fille du Pharaon* with Mordkin. Years later, with all their quarrels behind them, he recalled the occasion sentimentally: "I still treasure a souvenir of that glorious night. It is a bit of red ribbon that once entwined a wreath of flowers. The wreath was sent to me by Anna Pavlova on the night of our great opening. . . . I sent flowers to [her], she sent flowers to me, and I have always cherished that bit of ribbon that entwined the stems. Even today it is faintly redolent of the perfume of those blossoms, and as I hold it in my hands I can see again that dimly lit theatre and hear once more the ringing applause and the cries of 'Bravo!'" Even such an enthusiastic reception as this could not have prepared the two dancers for the tumults that would greet them in later years.

Pavlova and Mordkin danced together several more times before she returned to St. Petersburg. They didn't meet again until the first season of the Ballets Russes in Paris in 1909.

Serge Diaghilev's object in choosing dancers for his revolutionary new enterprise was the same as it had been when he organized art exhibitions: to cull from all over the country the very best Russia had to offer. It was natural that he would choose Pavlova from the Maryinsky and Mordkin from the Bolshoi as the finest representatives of their different schools.

For this first Paris season, Pavlova was meant to dance with Nijinsky, and Mordkin was hired to partner another Bolshoi dancer, Vera Karalli, but the two were reunited when Mordkin replaced Nijinsky at short notice in a charity matinee at the Paris Opéra. Victor Dandré, Pavlova's husband and manager, said the appearance was virtually impromptu and remembered that Pavlova "took a liking" to Mordkin. Dandré may not have known about the earlier appearances in Moscow.

Pavlova was already beginning to feel that she would be happier dancing on her own than continuing with Diaghilev, and when the agent Daniel Mayer arranged for her to appear as part of a music hall bill at the Palace Theatre in London, she asked Mordkin to be her partner.

The pair first gave a special command performance, also arranged by Mayer, at a private party given by Lady Londesborough for King Edward VII and Queen Alexandra. This was an honor both remembered with great

The Russian Dance

pleasure for the rest of their lives.

Olga Racster called Pavlova and Mordkin's first appearance at the Palace Theatre "a landmark in the history of the Russian ballet in this century." It was a landmark in the history of all ballet. A Palace Theatre program listing their performance promises "Varieties and Novelties." From the looks of the buxom girls on the cover, the dancers were in low company, but their art shone through. People who came for variety and novelty found instead a revelation. *The Tatler* for 1910 registered "an impression" for its readers: "For a few all-too-brief moments we saw the thing for which we are most of us searching all our lives—absolute incontestable beauty." The *Pall Mall Gazette* for 23 June 1910 noted how the popularity of the pair had exceeded the bounds of the theatrical world and become something of a national event:

"Have you seen Pavlova?

"The words have become almost a catch phrase. At the dinner tables or in the clubs, wherever two people meet together, the talk turns on Anna Pavlova and Mikhail Mordkin: the dancers from Russia, whose art is of a kind which has never before been seen in London.

"They have become a cult. People go to see them again and again. Their dancing is so wonderful it is not enough to see them once. Just as you could look forever on a beautiful picture, or never tire of the Venus de Milo, or read and re-read some masterpiece of literature, so the desire to see Anna Pavlova and Mikhail Mordkin is luring people of all classes to the Palace Theatre."

We see from this passage that Pavlova and Mordkin had restored dancing, which had become a dubious, tawdry spectacle in London, to its proper place beside great art and "masterpieces of literature," while at the same time appealing to an enormous range of people. This was one of their most important achievements. Their programs, which included selections from *Papillon, Valse Caprice,* and Petipa's *Autumn Bacchanale,* clearly startled critics who thought they knew all too well what dancing meant. "These Russian artists are not dancers in the conventional sense of the word: their art does not consist merely in pirouettes and entrechats. They act," conceded the *Daily News.* And the *Daily Mail* concurred. "It is none of the conventional tricks of the ballet dancer that causes wonderment in the dancing of Anna Pavlova and her no less amazing partner, but their extraordinary effects of movement arrested." They were the talk and the toast of the town. Sir Alfred Butt, owner of the Palace, said they achieved in a single night a greater success than any artist he could remember, and a special matinee was added to meet the audience demand.

The pair had the same dazzling success in New York, where they had been invited to dance at the Metropolitan Opera House by Otto Kahn. "New York . . . was prepared for any kind of a sensation except that in store—a whirlwind of pure artistry of a character unheard of here. . . . Twenty-four hours later society, art circles, music lovers, and the masses were aflame with enthusiasm."

Their first appearance was in a revival of *Coppélia,* given after a full-length performance of the opera *Werther.* Many of the audience remained to see them out of curiosity or politeness. By the second evening, word had spread, and they drew a record crowd and receipts up to $15,000—an astonishing figure in those days. At this second performance they offered two divertissements: the frenzied *Autumn Bacchanale* (in Olga Racster's words, "an orgy enveloped in the luscious red and

gold of autumn") and a breathtaking woodland adagio. Music critic Carl Van Vechten had seen them frolic through the gay and classical *Coppélia* and was impressed by their virtuosity. "Anyone who had seen their previous performance would have had difficulty in recognizing them," he wrote, and went on to describe the woodland piece's extraordinary finish: "Pavlova . . . swooped into the air like a bird and floated down. She never dropped. At times she seemed to defy the laws of gravitation. The divertissement ended with Pavlova, supported by Mordkin, flying through the air, circling his body around and around. The curtain fell. The applause was deafening." Agnes de Mille, to whom Pavlova was an inspiration, gave a characteristically flourishing account of the dancers' effect on the public: "[Pavlova] came to New York partnered by the first great male star of ballet this country had ever seen, and aroused a popular response no one in this century had commanded . . . women wept and ripped the violets out of their muffs and hurled them on the stage."

New York City had the same effect on the two dancers that they had on their public— dizzying and exhilarating. "Events piled one on another with incredible swiftness," Mordkin recalled. "We moved so rapidly that we were scarcely conscious of movement. . . . We were very happy and very busy and very tired." And Pavlova referred to New York as a "crazy wheel revolving with lightning-like rapidity."

The lightning wheel of fortune flung Pavlova and Mordkin into a second engagement at the Metropolitan Opera House, two strenuous American tours, and more London appearances. When they appeared at the Mews Theatre in London, it was sold out for the first time in its history, and audiences frequently waited long into the night to see them. Music hall performers took to copying them, parody being the sincerest form of flattery. In a London paper, a column called "At the Halls" noted, "At the Palace Messrs. Edmund Payne and George Grossmith will vary their 'turn' and introduce for the first time tomorrow their funny burlesque of Pavlova and Mordkin."

In America, Pavlova and Mordkin traveled to cities that had not seen ballet since Fanny Elssler toured in the 1840s, and the response was awestruck. Louis V. De Voe called them "that pair of ethereal geniuses," and the *Musical Courier* wrote, "Russian dancing has undoubtedly left an indelible imprint upon the American mind, largely due to the visitations of Pavlova and Mordkin." It was probably no accident that this writer chose the word "visitations," usually associated with religious revelations.

For the performers, touring was debilitating.

The Autumn Bacchanale. Cover, *The Play Pictorial.* Victoria and Albert Museum

Mordkin used to almost hypnotize Pavlova out of her exhaustion by whispering, "I know you are all right," and remembers the travel across country as a nightmare of socializing: "We watched children's dancing classes, we saw physical education exhibits, we attended benefits and bazaars, teas and receptions. We shook hands with artists and dancing teachers, merchants and politicians. We were photographed in every conceivable pose by zealous cameramen who seemed to pop out of every dark corner." The ballets suffered the usual indignities of touring, especially Mordkin's own Arabian Nights ballet *The Legend of Azyiade,* to a lush medley by Glazunov, which seemed to provide more than its fair share of embarrassment. Once, at the emotional peak of the ballet, Pavlova hurled herself into Mordkin's arms with what he dryly referred to as "her usual vigor," and the sofa

collapsed. Another time, in the absence of a trap door, Pavlova had to crouch, Houdini-like, in a small wooden box onstage while Mordkin danced.

Relations between the two dancers deteriorated throughout the 1911 season. There were probably faults on both sides. Pavlova was querulous and autocratic. As her biographer, Arthur H. Franks, noted, "Her personality and temperament demanded that she remain always the dominating figure." She tended to see a partner as someone to ornament her own attraction. Dance to her was a religion, and Mordkin was left with the ungraceful task of tending the chosen vessel. Mordkin, on the other hand, was obsessed by the question of billing and jealous of the adulation Pavlova received. In a story told by Theodore Stier, Pavlova's musical director, Mordkin's jealousy reached a hilarious apex over supper one evening, when Mordkin, purple with rage, thrust the menu at Pavlova and said, "There you are! Now you see! Frog's legs à la Pavlova! Always it is yourself! Never of Mordkin you think, but always Pavlova, Pavlova, Pavlova! Frog's legs à la Pavlova! But where is there frog's legs à la Mordkin? Where is anything eatable à la Mordkin? Tell me that."

These depressing squabbles reached a crescendo during the pair's final appearances at the Palace Theatre, when, after Mordkin dropped Pavlova in the *Autumn Bacchanale* and she slapped his face, they alternated between giving astonishing performances and refusing to appear together at all. One journalist described the atmosphere on the night of Mordkin's final appearance as "electric." At the close of the program there was an unseemly race for curtain calls. In the end Pavlova got the palm, as she has in history.

But history, too, has dimmed the details of their quarrels and highlighted instead their extraordinary achievements and genuine sympathies.

Alexandre Benois described Mordkin, not flatteringly, as "strong and vigorous," but it was those very qualities that audiences enjoyed and that made him a perfect foil for Pavlova's frail, incandescent femininity. Pavlova's face and form seemed to change with every role she danced, whereas Mordkin seemed carved in marble with rippling muscles, a classically straight nose, and abundant curly hair. They had the ability to make their particular beauties seem symbolic of eternal beauty. Pavlova was not merely pliant and reedlike but "the soul of soulless things," as Svetloff wrote; and Mordkin was not merely handsome but godlike, "a classic being, fired with the passion of centuries," as another writer put it.

Observers noted these contrasts and the fact that onstage the pair seemed to form a harmonious whole. "He is like an ancient statue come to life . . . she is the symbol of life and femininity and of beauty which is the soul of life." "Together they form a harmonious unit as smooth and frictionless as the quietly moving engine." "In the dance they seem indissoluble, the vital beauty of an Olympic victor and the delicacy and spells of eternal woman."

Their repertory was chosen to enhance the contrasting skills of Pavlova and Mordkin. It included the "Bluebird" pas de deux from *The Sleeping Beauty, Autumn Bacchanale, Valse Caprice, Egyptian Nights, Raymonda,* Mordkin's own ballet, *The Legend of Azyiade,* as well as *Coppélia* and *Giselle*. These two dancers, who had disliked the rigidity of classical ballet in Russia, were able to infuse these classical adagios and national dances with new meaning and spontaneity. "The

appeal of the Pavlova and Mordkin art is both to the merely sensuous instincts and to the quality of poetic imagination in the spectator. . . . Underlying poetic significance is seldom lacking." In ballets like *Giselle* and *Azyiade,* the pair exuded a kind of romantic inevitability that is one of the magical aspects of partnership. Pavlova was amazingly receptive to ideas and impressions, and offstage Mordkin would talk to her about the atmosphere of her parts to inspire her. He remembered describing "that shadowy land after death" to prepare her for *Giselle*.

Their gift for imparting meaning to the simplest gestures prompted comparisons with Isadora Duncan. Even their relatively simple pas de deux were such a revelation to critics like Carl Van Vechten that we can see these critics reaching not only for richer and richer superlatives but also for a correct aesthetic and technical vocabulary to encompass what they have seen. One writer, after seeing the woodland adagio, admits that "the stock of our adjectives is too weak to describe it."

Not all criticism took this high tone, however. In a facetious article, "The Afternoon of a Few Fauns," Michael Milholland called Pavlova and Mordkin "the first emissaries of ecstasy." And we are wrong to think *Cosmopolitan* was the first to view men as sex objects: Oleg Kerensky (in his biography of Pavlova) quotes this review by Algernon St. John-Brenon: "Mordkin's [legs] are particularly excellent. In certain companies they would be starred. Tacitly, I believe they are starred in this. They received a round of applause all to themselves when they came along with Mordkin safely fixed onto them holding a bow and arrow . . . the enthusiasm of the elderly ladies in the audience was remarkable. We imply nothing. We insinuate nothing. We are above innuendo."

Pavlova and Mordkin's most famous offering was Petipa's *Autumn Bacchanale*. This "revel of wine and sunshine and love, . . . full of the wildest and most sensuous delights of the wine cup and with a breathless activity that was the very essence of intoxication," fully expressed the dancers' technical brilliance and emotional abandon. "Whatever a person does or refrains from doing out of fear, is bad," Pavlova wrote, and the *Bacchanale* seemed to be their personal symbol of fearlessness. "Pavlova and Mordkin swept the audience almost literally out of their chairs," gasped one reviewer. They did more. For all who saw them, Pavlova and Mordkin swept away apathy about dancing and returned its poignancy and excitement. For us, as much as to those who were there, "Pavlova and Mordkin together . . . grave their memory upon the mind that will not be slow to forget them."

Tamara Karsavina & Vaslav Nijinsky

"Hundreds of eyes followed us about; scraps of exclamations: 'He is a prodigy' and 'C'est elle!' . . . I realized something immense was happening to me and around me; something to which I could give no name, so unexpected, so enormous as to frighten almost. My senses were all blurred on that night."

That night is 18 May 1909. It is the opening of the Russian Ballet at the Théâtre du Châtelet in Paris. The writer, Tamara Karsavina, has just danced in Fokine's *Le Pavillon d'Armide* with Vaslav Nijinsky and is astonished by the reaction backstage, where the audience has broken the barriers just to catch a glimpse of the extraordinary Russians. She is excited and alarmed. Nijinsky, wrapped in the character of Armida's Favorite Slave, is oblivious to the swelling crowds.

Soon the pair reappear and perform *L'Oiseau de Feu,* actually Petipa's "Bluebird" pas de deux, and the audience is overwhelmed. Backstage again, Karsavina is embraced by an ecstatic Serge Diaghilev. Her arm is bleeding where Nijinsky's tunic has cut it, but she is too dazed to notice. Nijinsky is politely explaining to an admirer that his prodigious leaping is not really difficult: "You have just to go up and to pause a little up there."

By the next morning Karsavina was "La Karsavina" and Nijinsky was the new Vestris and "God of the Dance." Serge Diaghilev's Ballets Russes, which would change the course of ballet, was launched and so was a remarkable and unanalyzable partnership between a glamorous and articulate woman and a mysterious, feral, and uncommunicative boy.

Paris was not, of course, Karsavina and Nijinsky's first meeting ground. Both attended

Duration of partnership: 1909–12
Companies: Maryinsky, Diaghilev Ballets Russes
Principal Ballets: *Carnaval, Cleopatra, Daphnis and Chloe, Giselle, Jeux, Narcisse, Le Pavillon d'Armide, Petrouchka, Le Spectre de la Rose*

Carnaval. Victoria and Albert Museum

Giselle

**"I am the wraith of a rose
You wore at the dance last night."
—Théophile Gautier**

the Imperial Ballet School in St. Petersburg, though Karsavina, several years Nijinsky's senior, was already a soloist with the Maryinsky when she first saw Nijinsky in class. It was a moment she would never forget: "One morning I came up earlier than usual; the boys were just finishing their practice. I glanced casually, and could not believe my eyes; one boy in a leap rose far above the heads of the others and seemed to hang in the air. 'Who is this?' I asked Mikhail Obukhov, his master. 'It is Nijinsky; the little devil never comes down with the music.' He then called Nijinsky forward by himself and made him show me some steps. A prodigy was before my eyes."

Karsavina, let in on the secret, as it were, took an interest in Nijinsky and perhaps for this reason was chosen to partner him in his coming-out performance. A special pas de deux was introduced into the program for them—it was probably the "Peasant" pas de deux from Act I of *Giselle.* From the first there was an unspoken sympathy between them, which Karsavina recalled in a series of articles for the *Dancing Times,* "My Partners at the Maryinsky." "As every dancer knows, double work needs above everything knowledge of each other's reactions and timing, which alone gives the dancer complete confidence.

"How much the interplay of personalities matters, I soon realized. In my fourth year on the stage, it was given to me to sponsor the coming out of Nijinsky . . . His master, Obukhov, coached him in the double work; but there was hardly any need for it—Nijinsky had an instinctive right touch in partnering. His hands, though small, had all the sensitiveness of antennae, anticipating his partner's every intent. Waiting in the wings, he would pad to and fro with that feline step peculiar to him, limbering his wrists and fingers."

When Diaghilev chose his dancers to appear in the first Russian season in Paris, Nijinsky was meant to partner Anna Pavlova rather than Karsavina. She was the more renowned of the two dancers in Russia and already a prima ballerina. But Pavlova arrived late for the season, and soon, except for a few brief appearances, disassociated herself altogether from the Ballets Russes, so Karsavina and Nijinsky entered history together.

Karsavina's childhood had been relatively prosperous and secure. Nijinsky's, with his half-witted brother and a mother deserted by her husband, was often full of want and uncertainty. Karsavina was confident and intellectual; Nijinsky, shy and introspective. But aside from their schooling, two powerful influences bound this unlikely pair together. One was Fokine, the other was Diaghilev.

Michel Fokine was revolutionizing ballet, substituting a lyric naturalism for the great unwieldy panoplies of Marius Petipa. Fokine's ballets, with the exception of *Les Sylphides,* tended to do away with traditional partnering, with the highly structured pas de deux form, but replaced it with a powerful atmosphere in which a partnership like Karsavina and Nijinsky's succeeded because of the dancers' ability to create and sustain a wide variety of moods and nuances of feeling. In writing of partners and partnering, Karsavina said that Fokine's ballets "made me realize that the inner cohesion between the two mattered as much as mere skill in supporting." There is evidence of this "inner cohesion" in all accounts of them. In *Cleopatra* they played two slaves, and Alexandre Benois described them as "two tender and carefree creatures." Fokine inserted, especially for them, a scarf dance, which might have been hackneyed with any other dancers. Karsavina, remembering it, paid another tribute to Nijinsky's partnering: "I

Le Spectre de la Rose

believe that with some other partner, less responsive to music, and not so supremely sensitive of the pattern of the dance as he was, my scarf might not have traced such a perfect curve in the horizontal lifts." Music was an important element in Fokine's ballets. He believed that "music isn't the mere accompaniment of a rhythmic step, but an organic part of a dance." Karsavina and Nijinsky were able to make themselves an organic part of the music. Of Nijinsky, Karsavina wrote, "That sense of music seemed to permeate his body. Nijinsky's dance was music made visible." Cyril Beaumont, recalling them in *Les Sylphides,* said, "I always think of Karsavina and Nijinsky as the perfect partners. . . . But these two were not mortals. It was the poet's shade visiting, in company with the spirit of his dead mistress, the moonlit grove which had once inspired his imperishable odes."

In addition to musicality, Fokine's ballets demanded of his dancers a tremendous versatility and protean quality. Impatient with the old tradition of mime, in which whole unassimilated chunks of plot would be semaphored to the audience, Fokine believed that gestures had an integrity of their own and should be able to convey ambiance and the essence of a character. Karsavina and Nijinsky had to an exceptional degree the ability to unite gesture with meaning and to transform themselves utterly in a role. Robert Brussel, a journalist for *Le Figaro* and an enthusiastic chronicler of the magic first seasons in Paris, described Karsavina as an "elusive, thoughtful beauty who seems wafted by infinite grace," and Nijinsky as "a kind of modern Vestris, but whose dazzling technique is allied to a plastic feeling and a distinction of gesture which are certainly unequalled anywhere." When Karsavina wrote of the Ballets Russes' first season in Paris, "Something akin to a miracle happened every night—the stage and the audience trembled in a unison of emotion," it was this quality they were responding to; and the choreographer himself paid tribute to it. Fokine was astonished by Nijinsky's ability to absorb himself in a role until he really changed before people's eyes: "He gradually began to change into another being, the one he saw in the mirror. He became reincarnated and actually *entered into* his new existence." And he marveled at the elusive simplicity of the Ballerina role in *Petrouchka,* which seemed to be just a matter of two blobs of rouge and false eyelashes but was never again portrayed as Karsavina portrayed her. Just as only Nijinsky could give credible feeling to a faun, a rose, only Karsavina could succeed at that baffling emptiness of heart. Karsavina wrote, "Most memorable and happy to me were Fokine's

productions in which Nijinsky and I created the leading roles," and she was particularly fond of *Petrouchka.* She describes vividly Nijinsky's virtual possession by the role, certainly the most poignant in his career. "I remember nostalgically another experience I shared with Nijinsky—*Petrouchka.* . . . It seemed to me that Nijinsky lived himself into that part, as it were. Usually uncommunicative, undemonstrative, he now, during the period of rehearsals, would impulsively jerk like a puppet or emit Petrouchka's cry."

During their partnership Karsavina and Nijinsky danced in almost every role in the Ballets Russes repertory, an astonishing range of characters and creatures. They were the carefree slaves in *Cleopatra,* lyric shades in *Les Sylphides,* and puppets in *Petrouchka.* Karsavina took over Ida Rubinstein's role of Zobeide in *Schéhérazade* and was a passionate object of desire for Nijinsky's exotic and feline Golden Slave. In *Carnaval,* the jolly *commedia dell'arte* characters became something more in the hands of these supreme interpreters. Karsavina's Columbine was the eternal coquette (fifty years later she would tell Richard Buckle, "I have that in my bones") and Nijinsky transformed Harlequin (though he was originally cast as Florestan) from something obvious into something elusive and mysterious. "A sly fellow," observed Geoffrey Whitworth, "slickly insinuating, naughtily intimate. He is always whispering subtle secrets to Columbine, and is saved from viciousness only by his unerring sense of fun. Certainly he is the most uncanny and least human of all Nijinsky's creations. For this Harlequin is the very soul of mischief—half Puck—but Puck with a sting and with a body like a wire of tempered steel." Even in Fokine's two Greek ballets, *Narcisse* and *Daphnis and Chloe,* which lacked the immediacy of his other works and were not great successes, Karsavina and Nijinsky were singled out for their beauty. In *Narcisse* they had a haunting pas de deux where Karsavina, as Echo, repeated Nijinsky's steps, which became progressively more and more elaborate. The action in both *Narcisse* and *Daphnis and Chloe* isolated or separated the partners and seems to indicate that the most successful ballets were those that offered some interaction between the two.

Perhaps their most famous ballet together was *Le Spectre de la Rose,* a cameo, a concentrated essence of wistful romance whose haunting fragrance lingers on over half a century later. "Ah, this *Spectre de la Rose,* they sigh, who saw it; and so complete had been its sway over the hearts, so subtly penetrating its fragrance, that they sigh as well who had missed the *Spectre de la Rose.*" That is Karsavina speaking, twenty years later, and she remembered that even the rehearsals for *Spectre* had a magical aura. "Fokine composed *Le Spectre* in one swoop of inspiration; Diaghilev watched, visibly pleased there was no one else to detract from the intimacy and loving concentration of that first rehearsal." Perhaps nowhere else did Nijinsky demonstrate so clearly his uncanny blend of the human and the inhuman, his ability to transform himself utterly into an imaginary being, and nowhere did Karsavina dance with such deceptive but inimitable simplicity. Valentine Hugo, whose drawings captured so many of Nijinsky's roles, described *Spectre* imaginatively: "The fluid grace of Tamara Karsavina, returned from the ball, weary and bemused by the noise, the faces, and the waltzes, leaning for a moment against the french window of her virginal room with the park beyond, then gently falling into an armchair, shrouded in the white mist of her flimsy dress, the red rose, a little faded, in her bodice. . . . Suddenly the music is hushed and through the top of the open window from the moonlit garden springs this aerial vision, unreal, not covered in roses, not a rose, but the very essence of a rose. . . .

"The spectators of this sorcery hardly dared to breathe for fear that this never-to-be-forgotten vision might vanish." The writer and artist Jean Cocteau was another enchanted spectator: "Exulting in his rosy ecstasy he seems to impregnate the muslin curtains and take possession of the dreaming girl." Nijinsky's wife Romola described Nijinsky's make-up, concocted by himself, which helped transform him inwardly as well as outwardly. "His face was like that of a celestial insect, his eyebrows suggesting some beautiful beetle which one might expect to find closest to the heart of a rose, and his mouth was like rose petals." Photographs recorded this extraordinary look and also recorded Karsavina, weightless in her filmy dress. Just as, in the role of Columbine, she was all coquettes, here she was all dreaming girls, and we can see in pictures the almost trancelike harmony between the two dancers—Karsavina wafting up into the limpid petal-like arms of the hovering Nijinsky. *Spectre* never looked like that again.

When the Ballets Russes came to London, a critic of *The Times* tried to analyze its devastating impact on the drowsy world of English ballet. "Our English ballets have had so little concern with the imagination that even the most pitiful little crumbs of imaginative food . . . have caused something of a flutter amongst us. And now that we have suddenly set before us the abundant fare supplied by the inventive genius of a Benois and a Fokine . . . and the interpretative genius of a Nijinsky, a Karsavina

. . . is it to be wondered at that we fall to so greedily? For here we are introduced to a whole range of ideas such as we have never met before." The writer makes a distinction between "creative genius"—choreographers—and "interpretative genius"—dancers—but we have seen that in many ways Karsavina and Nijinsky helped to create their roles, giving them shades of meaning that may have surprised even Fokine.

Of course, Fokine's were not the only ballets danced by Karsavina and Nijinsky, though he was the dominating influence. In addition to Petipa's "Bluebird" pas de deux (for which Diaghilev always seemed to be inventing new names), they danced in *Giselle* and in Nijinsky's *Jeux.* In fact, their only real quarrels were over these, one the oldest, the other, one of the most "modern" works in the repertory. Usually the two dancers' different approaches to their material, the one intellectual, the other instinctive, blended perfectly, but in the case of *Giselle,* Karsavina approached the sacrosanct classic in the traditional way and was disconcerted by Nijinsky's attempts to feel his way into the role by a show of antiheroic indifference. "I was sadly taken aback when I found that I danced, married, went off my head and died of a broken heart without any response from Nijinsky. He stood pensive and bit his nails." Eventually harmony was restored by Diaghilev; and while the ballet *Giselle* itself would not be popular until it flourished with another great partnership (that of Markova and Dolin), it was considered a triumph for its interpreters. A photograph shows Nijinsky, looking radiantly noble, supporting Karsavina in a deep backbend. She seems as supple and fearless as the ghost beyond all pain she is meant to be.

The case of *Jeux* was opposite to that of *Giselle.* Instead of Karsavina trying to enforce the old mime and the traditional conception, Nijinsky was attempting to explain to classically trained dancers an entirely new and dissonant conception of movement. Its dislocated movements and abstract structure would have made *Jeux* a difficult proposition anyway, but this was aggravated by the choreographer's inability to explain what he wanted. As Karsavina wrote, "Nijinsky had no gift of precise thought, still less that of expressing his ideas in adequate words." Tempers flared, but they died down, and what pictures we have of the piece tantalize us by their sculptured beauty and glimpse of mysterious personal relationships.

Offstage, Karsavina and Nijinsky were fast friends and frequent companions. In the frenzy at the Châtelet before the opening of the first season, in that whirlwind of scenery and blinis and rehearsals, they quietly practiced

Petrouchka

pirouettes in a corner. If Fokine was their link in performance, Diaghilev was their link in public life. He cherished them and took them everywhere, to suppers, parties, museums, and drives into the country, after which he would deliver them, late, to a cross Maestro Cecchetti for their private lesson. He drove them relentlessly and, writes Karsavina, "An equal frenzy of learning possessed both Nijinsky and myself."

The potent alchemy of the Ballets Russes changed not only ballet history but art and fashion, and artists were eager to capture the special magic of Karsavina and Nijinsky. Cocteau, Rodin, and Jacques-Émile Blanche were among the enthusiastic evokers of what one poster referred to as "the exquisite Karsavina" and "the incomparable Nijinsky." And they attracted the influential as well as the artistic. In England they were sponsored by Lady Ripon and Lady Ottoline Morrell; in Paris they danced for the Aga Khan and he invited them to India.

Nijinsky's marriage in 1913 (at which Karsavina made a beautiful speech) and his subsequent estrangement from the Ballets Russes separated the partners; and then the war and Nijinsky's madness cut him off finally from everyone, including himself. In one attempt to bring him to his senses, Diaghilev took him to a performance of *Petrouchka*, hoping that the sight of this role, which he had felt so deeply, would stir his memory. Karsavina, in her old role as the Ballerina, came to meet him and never forgot the heart-rending moment:

"I saw vacant eyes and a passive shuffling gait and stepped forward to kiss Nijinsky. A shy smile lit up his face, and his eyes looked straight into mine. I thought he knew me, and I was afraid to speak lest it might interrupt a slow-forming thought. He kept silent. I then called him by his pet name 'Vatza!' He dropped his head and slowly turned it away. Nijinsky meekly allowed himself to be led to where the photographers had set their cameras. I put my arm through his, and, requested to look straight into the camera, I could not see his movements. I noticed that the photographers were hesitating and looking around, I saw that Nijinsky was leaning forward and looking into my face, but on meeting my eyes he again turned his head like a child that wants to hide tears. And that pathetic, shy, helpless movement went through my heart."

When Nijinsky died in 1950, Lydia Sokolova wrote, "My heart ached for Madame Karsavina, whose beauty and fame were linked with his in a perfect harmony of dancing, which has never been surpassed." We are grateful now to those eager artists and to the writers of the passionate accounts for our glimpses of this perfect harmony, but some of it we must imagine. Karsavina and Nijinsky are at once with us, and part of our heritage, and lost to us forever. It is rather like Romola Nijinsky's description of the most famous moment in *Spectre de la Rose:* "With one soft kiss he gives her a part of the unattainable and then forever leaps into the infinite."

Alicia Markova & Anton Dolin

"Their greatness lies in their realization of an ideal, based on a lifetime of work."
—Vincenzo Celli

Duration of partnership: 1929–59 (intermittently)
Companies: Diaghilev Ballets Russes, 1929; Ballet Club, Camargo Society, Vic-Wells Ballet, all in the period 1931–35; Markova-Dolin Ballet, 1935–37; Ballet Theatre, 1941–45; London Festival Ballet, 1951–57; various concert groups throughout career
Principal Ballets: *Aucassin and Nicolette, The Beloved One, Giselle, The House Party, The Nightingale and the Rose, The Nutcracker, Swan Lake*

On New Year's Day, 1934, Alicia Markova and Anton Dolin became the first British couple to dance *Giselle*. This was a great moment for British ballet, then in its first flowering, but it was also the formal beginning of a partnership that was to delight audiences around the world for over twenty years. At the end of her book, *Giselle and I*, Markova writes: "That first moment: Albrecht's tap on the cottage door; the music's long tremor as we wait . . . and then, the joyous springing up of melody, as Giselle comes out to greet another morning, to meet another Albrecht . . ." More often than not, that Albrecht was Anton Dolin, but *Giselle* is only the most famous of the many ballets they danced together in a long and satisfying partnership.

In ballet terms, Markova and Dolin were childhood sweethearts. They met as fellow pupils at the studio of Princess Serafina Astafieva, when Markova was still a child and still Alicia Marks, and Dolin was laboring under the unballetic name of Sydney Francis Patrick Chippendall Healey-Kay. They were the most promising students in the class. In *Balletomania*, Arnold Haskell recalls: "I do not think that any of us who frequented the studio doubted for a moment that the boy, Pat, and little Alicia would make big names, and play their part in the main movement of ballet." Critics seemed to agree. When Astafieva's pupils appeared at the Royal Albert Hall, *The Dancing Times* singled out Markova and Dolin as the high points of the program: "Quite a feature of the evening was the really wonderful *Dance Russe* by Anton Dolin . . . I do not like 'Dying Swans,' but really that by Little Alicia . . . was decidedly good."

Anton Dolin remembers that he and Markova used to practice together at Astafieva's, and that she was very easy to work with ("We did a lot of showing off . . . she did triple tours—I could have killed her at times."), but it was really Diaghilev and his Ballets Russes that provided the alchemy that both changed their names and transformed them as dancers.

In the Ballets Russes Dolin, some years older than Markova, was like an older brother to her, loving, clucking, scolding, fussing about her clothes and her bedtime. In some ways he

"Bluebird" pas de deux. Photo: Courtesy John Travas/London Festival Ballet

Casse Noisette. Photo: Courtesy John Travas/London Festival Ballet

never lost this attitude. When he talks about her he often sounds protective and indulgent, and in one of his volumes of autobiography he comments "Alicia was like a sister, and a divine dancing partner."

Markova and Dolin did not actually perform together until Diaghilev's last London season, at Covent Garden in 1929. There they danced the "Bluebird" pas de deux in the company's lavish and ill-fated production of *The Sleeping Princess*. Diaghilev died soon after. The decade following his death and the dissolution of the Ballets Russes saw the foundation of British ballet and the consolidation of Markova's and Dolin's stardom and partnership.

Together and separately, they performed with Marie Rambert's Ballet Club, with the Camargo Society, and its offspring, the Vic–Wells Ballet. As the Vic–Wells first stars, Markova and Dolin made an inestimable contribution to the founding of a national company and the finding of a national style. Audiences flocked (as much as audiences ever flocked to ballet in those days) to see them in *Swan Lake* Act II, in *Casse Noisette* and Ashton's *The Lord of Burleigh*. Individually, Dolin thrilled as the demonic Satan in Ninette de Valois's *Job*, and Markova enchanted in *Les Rendezvous*, *Façade*, and *The Haunted Ballroom*. Between these times Dolin, a theatrical polyglot, toured with Vera

Giselle. Photo: Courtesy John Travas/London Festival Ballet

Nemchinova and appeared with Gertrude Lawrence, Argentinita, and Harry Richman in "International Revue." A 1950 *Dance and Dancers* article sums up their contribution to ballet in England: "They were the foundation stones of the Vic–Wells Ballet . . . from the onset we had a model that was, and still is, considered to be the high watermark of classical ballet performance."

The day of the historic *Giselle* performance approached. Dolin had danced the ballet before, with Olga Spessivtseva at the Camargo Society, and proved to be a perfect coach for Markova. She had watched Spessivtseva in the role, so, as with their early schooling and Ballets Russes experience, the pair were once again drawing inspiration from the same source. In an article about this first *Giselle* Markova recalled Dolin as "a perfect partner." His own reminiscences are more pungent: "It was the foggiest day in England. We both said, 'Can there be an audience on this ghastly night?'" There was, and they were ecstatic, but Dolin himself was the first to comment, with that pleasurable objectivity about Markova's extraordinary talents he retained throughout their joint career: "Markova's performance in *Giselle* has proved her, at the early age of twenty-three, worthy to rank with all the greatest artistes. She has something she will find it difficult to surpass." One first-night critic put his finger on an important reason for their success when he wrote "no two artists could have shown greater feeling and affection for this ballet." It is not exaggerating to say the *Giselle* owes its current popularity to the tremendous effort Markova and Dolin made to promote it all over the world, and to the particular beauty of their performances. "We did pioneer *Giselle*," Dolin asserts. "In those early days it was not a popular ballet. It took a long time. Sol Hurok said 'Why touch *Giselle?* It's box office poison.' Together, the two of us definitely did make *Giselle* one of the most popular ballets in the world. Perhaps this was our greatest triumph. We were unified . . . each giving to the other something that perhaps was unique and wonderful in this particular ballet." Observers amplified this feeling. "Her fragility and ethereal lightness is admirably set against his perfect partnering." wrote one. Mary Clarke, in her history of Sadler's Wells, mentions Markova's "quality of intangibility" and Dolin's "warm and living" Albrecht. Cyril Beaumont described their Act II adagio as "two voices singing in unison." Markova's phenomenal lightness, and Dolin's invisible support, became legendary. "Why, she's milkweed down," was the homey comment of one Chicago fan. "We get no thanks for what we do" was Dolin's humorous aside on the art of unobtrusive lifting.

Of course, in a quarter-century of performances, there were bound to be some mishaps, and *Giselle* did not always have the requisite flawless, gossamer quality. Once, on tour in Birmingham, Markova fell flat on her back in Act II and lay with her legs and lilies pointing straight up, like a china lawn dog, while indulging in some very unspirit-like giggles. And in a Dallas auditorium the stage was so slippery an exasperated Dolin came forward and announced "Ladies and gentlemen, we are doing our best and trying to stand up, but neither Miss Markova nor I nor our group are billed to appear as The Ice Capades!"

But these were small adventures in a long string of moving and memorable performances. Perhaps the pair's absolute naturalness and conviction was the most memorable thing about them. "From the moment of their entrance, you knew they were right," wrote one critic, and Cyril Beaumont lay down the conditions they fulfilled so admirably for so long: "A romantic ballet demands a style of dancing and mime which breathes romance, and a nobility of manner; if these qualities be absent, there can be no romantic ballet."

In 1934 *Giselle* and its interpreters were just beginning their long journey. The following year Markova and Dolin formed the Markova-Dolin Ballet under the management of Vivian Van Damm, and toured all over England, promoting ballet and doing much to overcome the prejudice against English dancers. "Though Markova and Dolin are natives of these islands," runs an *Observer* piece "they could hardly have danced better or been more loudly cheered had they been Moscow graduates or Hollywood's latest humbugs." One member of the small company was Frederic Franklin, who would later develop an illustrious partnership of his own with Alexandra Danilova.

The first of the stars' touring groups to surmount all obstacles on the path to performance, the Markova-Dolin Ballet appeared in an amazing variety of circumstances and environments. In *Giselle and I*, Markova recalls being amused when *New York Times* critic John Martin wrote that she could make Giselle magical even in an "abandoned warehouse"—it was probably the only place she *hadn't* danced. Like Pavlova before them, Markova and Dolin felt they were bringing ballet to everyone, that performing classical roles and retaining a classical style in all conditions was not only inevitable, but healthy for their art. They deplored the rarified snobbery that looked down on their ventures into music halls, revues, and stadiums. "Never minded it at all," says Dolin. "Loved it. I like theatre. We were awfully criticised, Markova and I. Everyone thought it was *dreadful*. We

Les Biches. (The House Party) Photo: Courtesy John Travas/London Festival Ballet

were prostituting our art, etc., etc. Thank goodness all that snobbishness and nonsense is gone." Among the pair's strange bedfellows were such curiosities as "Mary and Erik: Rhythm and Wheels," "March of the Musketeers," and "Leonard Henry The Famous Wireless Star" at a performance at the London Coliseum. They danced in stadiums and arenas from the Hollywood Bowl to Haifa, but critics were quick to notice how strict their canons were: "With artists like Markova and Dolin, who refuse to appeal by stunts, ballet will never degenerate into mere spectacle." "Their performance was purely classical, restrained and beautifully finished."

Pushing back the frontiers of ballet could be hazardous. Many of the places where Markova and Dolin performed were entirely unprepared for ballet, and circumstances varied from the merely inconvenient to the positively treacherous. One stage was so rotten that their pianist fell through the floorboards and they had to dance blithely around a gaping hole. In Haifa, the theatre was open air, and they had to improvise an ending for Act I of *Giselle* to allow Markova to get to her dressing room. They carried her off the stage a decorous corpse; Markova says this gambit was made easier by the fact that she had contrived to knock herself out in her death fall. Dolin says when she got to her dressing room there was a snake in it. In Haifa there was at least the compensation that their audience was large enough to stretch far into the hills and taper into the stars. "Never a dull moment in the ballet," says Dolin, putting all their tempests into a philosophical teapot. "Never a dull moment in the ballet with Markova."

The Markova-Dolin Ballet's resident choreographer was Bronislava Nijinska, with whom both dancers had worked in the Ballets Russes. Among the ballets she did for them were *Autumn Song, The Beloved One,* and a revival of *Les Biches* under the title *The House Party. The Beloved One* was a romantic ballet, something like Ashton's *Les Rendezvous,* in which Dolin played a pianist and Markova his muse and vision of all the people in his life. He remembers her as being especially lovely in this piece. *The Beloved One,* like much of their concert repertory over the years, was designed to exploit Markova's remote, romantic impression and Dolin's vital dramatic stage presence. The program also included pieces which showed the pair off separately. Dolin staged Pavlova's *Dying Swan* for Markova, and he danced his own *Hymn to the Sun* (hilariously described in one program as being "redolent of sun-scorched wild thyme"). They catered to romanticism with *Les Sylphides* and *Giselle,* and more modern pieces like Wendy Toye's *Aucassin and Nicolette* and Dolin's *The Nightingale and The Rose.* The purely classical element was represented by *Swan Lake, Casse Noisette,* and the "Bluebird" pas de deux from *Sleeping Beauty.* All of which goes to prove that, though the Markova-Dolin legend has crystallized around *Giselle,* they were tremendously versatile dancers. Caryl Brahms paid homage to this first joint venture: "The line, the lightness, and the controlled flame that is the very essence of Alicia Markova's dancing; the fine theatre sense, the superb stage presence—the authority that Anton Dolin brings to the ballet; and their combined feeling for the tears which lie behind, and which perfect all beauty, lend to the company a unique distinction."

After the breakup of the Markova-Dolin Ballet in 1937, the dancers suspended their partnership for a short time, but were reunited in the United States, first for a single performance of *Giselle* at the Metropolitan Opera House, in 1940, and then as stars of the fledgling Ballet Theatre, where they would once again be "foundation stones" for a new and important national company. With *Giselle* as their staple offering (Dolin had staged the work for Ballet Theatre), Markova and Dolin conquered a new generation and a new continent. In addition to their appearances with Ballet Theatre they toured the United States, Central America and Mexico with a small concert group, sponsored by long-time admirer Sol Hurok. They both have fond memories of Mexico, where an adoring audience was supported by a reverent orchestra who played during their numerous curtain calls to honor them, and where there were so many of Markova's favorite flower, gardenias, that Dolin sent her a pillow of them after their first *Giselle.*

Touring in America was not noticeably more glamourous or sumptuous than in England, as witness this entry in Dolin's diary, written while Ballet Theatre was waiting for a bus to Miami: "The time is now one twenty a.m. Markova is lying stretched out on the pavement, using as mattress three overcoats which belong to Jerome Robbins, Johnny Kriza, and me, and her hat-box for a pillow." A more restful

interlude was provided by the Jacob's Pillow Festival the two organized in the summer of 1941. Time was spent teaching and performing, and, much to the astonishment of visiting journalists, cooking and cleaning. They gave a program called "The Age of Romantic Ballet" with representative material. Dolin had already enshrined Markova's Romantic and ethereal qualities in his version of *Pas de Quatre* for Ballet Theatre. At Jacob's Pillow he choreographed a *La Sylphide*-inspired pas de deux, *Taglioni and the Scotsman,* which Walter Terry described as "a duet which revealed that great ballerina magic which Markova possesses and the tender, yet strong, partnering of Dolin." A favorite photograph was taken, with Markova, in her sylph's costume, alighting in some silver birch trees.

The Nutcracker. Photo: Houston Rogers

In 1949 Markova and Dolin returned to England to dance *Giselle* at Covent Garden with the Sadler's Wells Ballet. They were widely acclaimed by a whole generation of dancers and ballet-goers to whom they were household names but unknown quantities. The *Dancing Times* reported "Markova has retained her amazing lightness and flow of movement . . . Anton Dolin, still dancing brilliantly, remains the perfect partner." And Cyril Beaumont cited them as an inspiration to younger dancers, observing "In Dolin, Markova has an ideal partner, for their long and successful stage partnership enables them to dance as one, with a perfect understanding of each other's movements and in complete sympathy."

The Covent Garden performance was followed by others, and by more tours in England and abroad. In South Africa they discovered a "Markova-Dolin Cocktail" had been invented in their honor. In 1950, with Dr. Julian Braunsweg, they founded the London Festival Ballet. It has become England's second largest and most prestigious company, so that the influence of Markova and Dolin now bestrides the English ballet world like a Colossus.

Alicia Markova and Anton Dolin last danced together in 1959, but their legend remains potent. A typically lush Hurok program note announces that "the stars of Alicia Markova and Anton Dolin have always been congruent. Today they seem to have become one." The critics agreed. What produced this extraordinary congruency?

In part it was the result of a sympathy born of common training and experience, but this was enhanced by a dovetailing of ideas and approaches, by perfect timing, by a nourishing contrast of personalities, and by some unanalyzable chemistry that produced what Bernard Sobel called "two souls with but a single ballet step." Physically, they both had dark vivid coloring, as if their features had been painted with single brush strokes, but Dolin was compact, muscular and bold, with a natural hauteur, while Markova exuded intensity and fragility.

"I think the most important thing in dancing with Markova," says Dolin "the great thing about our partnership—and I'm really quoting Sol Hurok—was that I gave out the feeling, to the audience, that this was the only person in the world that mattered to me. Markova is not exactly what I would call a very 'sexy' dancer, though not cold, either. I gave her what she gave me. I was exuberant and she was retired, and the two things blended very well together." Dolin's passion made Markova's ethereality seem more accessible and desirable, and her spirituality in turn enobled his feelings. Together they symbolized one of ballet's, particularly Romantic ballet's, oldest concerns: the meeting of the human and spiritual elements in nature.

Dolin has been acclaimed as one of the greatest partners in the history of ballet. "To be a good partner, fundamentally you've also got to love *being* a partner." Dolin insists. "I loved partnering, and I loved showing off my ballerina." To both dancers partnering was not a passive chore, but a creative and constructive skill. "She is the performance, I am, as it were, only a spectator" Dolin writes of adagio work, but it was often a performance he had helped to stage himself, as a *New Yorker* profile of Markova pointed out: "Skillfully giving her her head, he watches her with an apparently naive and unassumed delight which onlookers find contagious." Markova, discussing their work on *Giselle,* writes: "Albrecht is no mere foil to Giselle. A weak hero, far from helping the ballerina to shine in solitary glory, can upset the balance of the whole." Dolin, of course, was an actor of considerable force. Physical sympathy, too, counts for a good deal in partnering. Dolin says that, because he had always been able to dance on pointe easily, he appreciated the ballerina's work the more, and tried to enhance it. Markova, as it happens, was also able to do many of the traditionally "masculine" steps, such as multiple turns, and this may have given her a similar empathy with her partner.

In *Ballet Go Round* Dolin writes "I have always contended that a mental union between the two partners is the first and foremost step to a perfect partnership," and in *Giselle and I* Markova says "A partnership should be so close in mutual understanding that all technical points, even perfect timing, are taken for granted." Markova and Dolin had this "union"—an uncanny coincidence of feeling— to a remarkable degree. Of their work on character Markova says "to me he becomes Albrecht or Armand . . . when I'm studying I know just where he is going to meet me." This sympathy spilled over from, or into, their off-stage relationship, and Bernard Sobel was captivated by it: "They become excited over their reciprocal opinions. They ask and answer as if they were just discovering each other. One waits, tense and silent, while the other explains or expatiates. There is a deep mutual respect. The concordance is gracious and winning." "No two dancers have perhaps ever become as interwoven and united in their art," echoes A. V. Coton. It was this "concordance," aside from their considerable technical abilities, that moved audiences. Its result was complete sincerity in performance. "To go to a Markova-Dolin performance is not merely to escape from harsh reality . . . it is discovery. It is truth."

Alexandra Danilova & Frederic Franklin

"What I had with Danilova—the illumination she made for me—is imperishable."
—Frederic Franklin

"To take the steps and make them speak of love."
—Walter Terry

The efforts of America's pioneer settlers to tame the continent were almost equaled in scope and heroism by the exertions of Sergei Denham's Ballet Russe de Monte Carlo as it toiled back and forth across the country. For nearly fifteen years the mainstays of the company were Alexandra Danilova and Frederic Franklin. They formed a partnership of tremendous élan and vitality, particularly in the later years.

Danilova and Franklin's very different backgrounds prepared them well for the demands of the grueling Ballet Russe tours—requiring as they did a combination of endurance, versatility, and grace. Danilova was a graduate of the Imperial Ballet School and, with George Balanchine, a member of Diaghilev's Ballets Russes in its final years. She danced in everything from strictly classical works like *Swan Lake* to Balanchine's revolutionary *Apollon Musagète* (which we know today as *Apollo*). In Paris, she met people like Misia Sert and Coco Chanel.

Franklin came to ballet from quite a different route. He was born in Liverpool (he changed his name from Frederick to Frederic after the actor Fredric March—although he spelled it differently—but Danilova called him "Fredinka") and went to Paris as part of a music hall "turn" called The Lancashire Lads. In Paris, *he* met people like Josephine Baker and Mistinguett.

Duration of partnership: 1938–57
Companies: Ballet Russe de Monte Carlo, 1938–51; Metropolitan Ballet, 1949; Sadler's Wells Ballet, 1949; Slavenska-Franklin Ballet, 1952–55 (intermittently); concert tours
Principal Ballets: *Le Beau Danube, Coppélia, Danses Concertantes, Le Diable s'Amuse, Gaîté Parisienne, Mozartiana, The Nutcracker*

"Black Swan" pas de deux. Photo: Courtesy of *Dancing Times*

Gaîté Parisienne. Photo: Courtesy of *Dancing Times*

Coppélia. Photo: Victoria and Albert Museum

He then joined Wendy Toye (later a well-known British show choreographer) for a series of revues and was spotted there by Anton Dolin, who engaged him for the newly formed Markova-Dolin Ballet. When this dissolved in 1937, Franklin was invited by Léonide Massine to join Denham's Ballet Russe. Franklin would later write, "The best of me, as a dancer, is from a distillation of four great dancers: Markova and Dolin, Danilova and Massine. Each of them was unique."

Franklin's experiences in Paris and London had made him used to "dash," as he put it, in partners, and he couldn't have asked for more than he got in Alexandra Danilova, with her witty legs and lively personality, who had defected from René Blum's rival Ballet Russe in 1938. Franklin did not have her all to himself at first. Until the mid-1940s, Massine, Igor Youskevitch, and André Eglevsky were all active in the company, but when Franklin did get his chance a cherished ambition was realized. Franklin had first seen Danilova in 1929 in Diaghilev's production of *Aurora's Wedding,* and he had fallen in love: "I cut her picture out of the program and put it up on a wall over my bed. She was the most glamorous being imaginable. Danilova was then, as she was always to be, the epitome of 'the ballerina.'" He vividly recalls the beginning of their partnership: "I had begun rehearsing

Gaîté Parisienne and one day Massine came along and told me I would be dancing with Danilova. He had made me premier danseur of the company, Danilova's partner. It was the most impossible dream come true!"

In the days when the Monte Carlo was touring, dreams were something that had to be worked at. The company's enormous and exhausting tours sometimes covered as many as one hundred cities, with one- or two-night stands in each one, and barely enough time to get on a train before it was time to get off. Once, in Canada, they found an entire city snowbound and had to be taken from the railroad to the hotel in horse-drawn sleighs with bells on them. Appropriately enough, when George Balanchine became the company choreographer in 1944, the whole troupe appeared in the musical *Song of Norway.*

Leon Danielian remembers the Monte Carlo tours simply as "insane." Agnes de Mille, who traveled with them while choreographing *Rodeo,* brings to the experience a keener and more ironic eye: "They jog on together in the stewing untidy [train] cars. On arrival everyone frantically stuffs belongings into bags and boxes . . . Danilova unpins last night's orchids from the back of her seat. The poker players settle their debts rather loudly. Wet wash is stuffed into hat boxes, knitting into the cosmetics. All, girls and boys, load up and stagger out. There are not arms enough for gallantry and no one can afford a porter; the girls lug their own suitcases. The car looks like an abandoned picnic ground. The porter, untipped, is not charmed."

In the middle of this chaos, everyone remembers, Danilova and Franklin were troupers. Amiable, but with strong personalities, they "went to battle" (in Danielian's words) when the cause seemed just. They combined glamour and stoicism, the "grace under pressure" by which Dorothy Parker defined heroism. Agnes de Mille's first image of the Ballet Russe de Monte Carlo, as she approached the studio with trepidation to rehearse *Rodeo,* gives us a glimpse of Danilova and Franklin in action: "As I walked down the flowering drive I heard the music of *Gaîté* and a good deal of stamping and shouting. Shoura Danilova and Freddie Franklin were standing on chairs yelling the counts and clapping. The men, the great thick-muscled men, and the stringy-muscled girls were stamping and swooping and clenching their fists in a miasma of sweat. It was not a very large room and Shoura and Freddie were up to their waists in Parisian abandon."

In addition to dancing with the Monte Carlo, Danilova and Franklin appeared as guests with the Metropolitan Ballet, where they danced the "Black Swan" pas de deux (the *Dancing Times* said Danilova's "aplomb" was notable but Franklin's style was "eccentric"). They also appeared with the Sadler's Wells Ballet at Covent Garden in 1949.

Danilova gave her farewell performance with the Ballet Russe de Monte Carlo in Houston on 30 December 1951. Although, like many ballet partings, this separation of Danilova and Franklin proved to be only temporary, Franklin still remembers it as a great wrench: "The great trauma of those later years was in separating from Danilova. . . . It happened that we were all on the same railway platform that day, the company getting on a train going north, Danilova on a train going south. We behaved very bravely but I felt as though I were bleeding inside—as I watched Danilova's train pull out of the station I knew that a part of me had been torn away, and was gone forever."

Not forever, as it happened. The following year Franklin, too, left the Monte Carlo and co-founded his own company, the Slavenska-Franklin Ballet, with Yugoslavian ballerina Mia Slavenska. Danilova was a frequent guest star with the company, always warmly received. Later, the pair toured South America and Japan and appeared on television, preserving their old art in this new medium. In 1957, they were reunited with their old company, the Monte Carlo, for several guest appearances

and were praised for "their special elegance and exhilaration."

The Ballet Russe de Monte Carlo had a large and varied repertory, and Danilova and Franklin were equal to it. Their different backgrounds made both of them exemplary stylists and theatrical chameleons. One of the most formative influences on the two dancers and on their partnership was the work of Léonide Massine, for some years the leading choreographer of the company.

In an article about Massine, Dale Harris described the kind of dancer best suited to his work: "large in gesture, dramatically vivid, confidently individual." These were qualities exhibited to an extraordinary degree by Danilova and Franklin, making them as successful in Massine's colorful, satirical ballet bouffes as Karsavina and Nijinsky before them had been in Fokine's lush and fantastical productions.

The two Massine ballets for which Danilova and Franklin are best remembered are *Gaîté Parisienne* and *Le Beau Danube.* In each, a member of the privileged classes (Franklin) is romantically involved with a seductive lower-class girl (Danilova); and in each, the crowning moment is a waltz.

In *Gaîté* Franklin played a Baron (though Massine made him rehearse all the male roles and didn't tell him which he was doing until the last moment) in love with a vivacious Glove-Seller. In one performance described by Walter Terry, "The audience applauded at frequent intervals and accorded Alexandra Danilova an ovation on her entrance as the coquettish Glove-Seller. A warranted ovation it was, for this great ballerina danced the role to perfection. . . . Frederic Franklin was the romantic Baron and with Danilova stopped the show at the conclusion of their 'Grande Valse.'" Claudia Cassidy of the *Chicago Journal of Commerce* wrote of "Danilova the enchanting Glove-Seller and Franklin a Baron with élan." When the pair was reunited with Massine for a revival of *Gaîté* in 1951, Anthony Fay reported that "Danilova and Franklin glided through their old *Parisienne* portrayal and romantic reveries and memories prevailed." The two were able, with the depth of their characterizations, to suggest rounded characters with pasts and futures outside their moments on the stage. This was especially true in *Le Beau Danube*— "a ballet," wrote Walter Terry, "with which they are closely identified in the hearts and memories of all dance lovers."

The romance in *Le Beau Danube* is more complex and poignant than in *Gaîté.* Danilova's Street Dancer is hard and unsentimental—"a beautiful shrew," as Arnold Haskell described her (and it was in this ballet that he noticed Danilova's "magnificently straight knees") until she encounters the Hussar, an episode from her past who is engaged to marry a young girl of his own class. Their waltz together is a moment suspended in time—an idyllic recollection of a past they cannot recapture. The dance, alternating between flirtatious abandon and sculpted formality, seems to have epitomized the relationship between these two dancers who moved so easily from character dancing to classicism. Massine called Danilova "champagne on the stage" in this ballet, and Walter Terry observed that "dancing together, they worked their familiar magic as they moved, sometimes gently, and sometimes exuberantly, but always romantically to the strains of the Strauss music." Danilova herself may have pinpointed what made these two ballets so special to this partnership when she told John Gruen, "Love is never permanent, but art is permanent." It was as if these characters, as danced by Danilova and Franklin, used dancing as a way of fixing emotions that are otherwise ephemeral, so that with them dancing was not merely what people do in ballets, but completely and believably what people do. Danilova, with a curious distance from her role, says that she didn't like the vulgarity of the Street Dancer until she "began to see that she had a soul"—but it was Danilova who gave her that soul.

Gaîté and *Le Beau Danube* were popular works, but Danilova and Franklin enhanced even Massine's less distinguished pieces. Both were singled out for praise in reviews of *The New Yorker,* an oddball ballet based on the famous magazine's cartoons, which was meant to be New York City's *Gaîté* but fell rather flat. "In the large cast Danilova and Franklin were distinguished. The former for her serene artistry, the latter for his experience as a 'hoofer' which gave him a sense of style not shared by most of the company," wrote one critic. The pair also appeared as slick and volatile Spaniards in the Warner Brothers film *Spanish Fiesta,* based on Massine's *Capriccio Espagnol.*

Other choreographers were quick to exploit the pair's talents. Frederick Ashton made *Le Diable s'Amuse* especially for Danilova, and Franklin supported her with flair. Walter Terry had reservations about the piece, but praised its stars. "Danilova's sure sense of characterization and her humor would make any ballet in which she participated worth seeing." He thought Franklin, as The Young Lover, displayed "a robustness and a healthy athleticism." Edwin Denby enjoyed Danilova's "zip, humor, and technical facility," and said that Franklin's "unfailing energy, ability and communicable good humor constitute one of the ballet's greatest assets."

Massine had two successors as principal choreographer for the Ballet Russe de Monte Carlo: Bronislava Nijinska, who created *Chopin Concerto* on Danilova and Franklin, and George Balanchine, whose works *Danses Concertantes, Mozartiana,* and *Pas de Deux* (a divertissement to miscellaneous music from *The Sleeping Beauty*) seemed at once to be tailor-made for his stars and to require them to extend their abilities to the utmost.

Danses Concertantes, with its Stravinsky score, black-and-white set, and exciting jet-bedizened costumes, seemed as bright as the modern age and entirely suited, according to Anthony Fay, to Danilova and Franklin's "impulsive dance natures and techniques." Edwin Denby saw this impulsiveness channeled into character. "The stars whose happy flirtation is the central theme of the piece—and a birdlike duet it is—characterized their parts charmingly and lightly—he with the fatuousness of the happy male, she with the willfulness of a tender woman." They were "lightly natural comedians."

Mozartiana called forth from Denby his most detailed analysis of the two dancers' special qualities: "A ballerina's noble clarity of execution, her mastery over the many resources of dance rhythm, can make her formal steps and phrases seem poignantly unique and spontaneous, like a happy event in real life." Danilova was, in short, "a very great ballerina." "Franklin, Danilova's partner, danced with his happy flow of dance vitality and his wonderful generosity as a partner." Franklin says, "I adored the Russians for their passion—the intensity with which they loved dancing," and it is clear from Denby's observations that Franklin had absorbed this passion. "Franklin's dancing always makes perfect sense; like a true artist, he is completely at the service of the role he takes, and his straightforward delight in dancing, his forthright presence and openhearted nature give his version of the great classic roles a lyric grace that is fresh." Of *Pas de Deux,* Denby wrote, "When you see these two stars dancing beautifully on the stage you want them to go on dancing . . . their intimacy is that of young people in love and engaged, and their dance figures express the dewiness, the sense of trepidation in the girl, and the generous strength of the man."

Danilova and Franklin were among the forgers of the post-Diaghilev ballet world, but they also had considerable success in classics. They appeared together in *Giselle* and *Swan Lake,* in the pas de deux from *Nutcracker* and an early revival of *Raymonda,* but most of all they are remembered for *Coppélia,* which was to their classical repertory what *Gaîté Parisienne* and *Le Beau Danube* were to the modern.

The Red Poppy. Photo: Maurice Seymour

Raymonda. Photo: Maurice Seymour

It has been said that anyone who can dance *Coppélia* can dance anything. This comic masterpiece requires considerable dramatic ability, musicality, and wit, as well as the ability to dance, with no sense of strain, its very demanding classical passages. Danilova and Franklin are among the most celebrated exponents in the ballet's long history. Anthony Fay called them "a most provocative pair," and Denby found them nearly ideal. "Alexandra Danilova, incomparably brilliant in coquetry, wit, warm feminine graces and warm intelligence, was last night miraculous in classic clarity, in subtlety of rhythm, in daring and soaring elevation, in the biting edge of her toe steps and the wide, strong line of her wonderful extensions. . . . the elegance of her playfulness in this act and in the second were that of a peerless ballerina. . . . Franklin as the hero shone happily with the incomparable vitality he has and in classic passages he was clean in style, manly and imaginative." Among the many who saw and loved them in *Coppélia* was the young Lynn Seymour, who was inspired by their performance to become a dancer.

Danilova and Franklin were perfectly suited in every way. They had strong characters, but were infinitely adaptable; great comic gifts, as well as what Denby called "the gentle grand manner." When we see them dancing on film, they seem to feel the music in the same buoyant way, and their bodies are naturally in harmony. There is a sense of spaciousness and precision about their dancing; they have ample time to clarify each image for the audience. "Expressionism in movement must not be done with the face, but with the body," writes John Gruen, and Danilova and Franklin had two of the most expressive bodies in ballet. Like Markova and Dolin, they had similar coloring which took different and complementary forms. Franklin, dark, lean, and eager, looked like Sean Connery in the early James Bond films—a humorous swashbuckler. Danilova had a ripe, sensuous face, described by Tamara Geva as "Biblical" and by George Bernard Shaw as looking like "the young Queen Victoria" (not to be confused with the puglike old Queen Victoria). Recalling their partnership, Franklin says, "What I had with Danilova—the illumination she made for me—is imperishable."

Danilova and Franklin's partnership seems to have been above all things a study of romance. They portrayed lovers young and old, happy and tragic, recollecting and anticipating. In their long career they achieved— imperishably—one of the highest aims of the pas de deux, which is, in Walter Terry's words, "to take the steps and make them speak of love."

"He had the natural manner of a
danseur noble."
                    —Alicia Alonso

"As a dancer, to me I feel she was an
ideal partner."
                    —Igor Youskevitch

Alicia Alonso & Igor Youskevitch

Every once in a while, a dancer will appear who joins the two sides of traditional ballet: its technical bravura and its romanticism. Alicia Alonso and Igor Youskevitch were two such dancers, and their partnership combined scintillating technique with dramatic color and lyric grace. Alonso was a sylph, but she was a sylph of steel, and Youskevitch was a cavalier by birth and an athlete by training.

Both dancers came from good families and had superimposed on a natural delicacy of manner the rigorous schooling of the Imperial Ballet School in St. Petersburg, whose indirect heirs they were.

Alicia Alonso was born in Havana and began dancing as a child, but only for recreation, as was proper for a girl of good breeding. Her family was very much set against the idea of her embracing ballet as a career, and Alicia demonstrated the revolutionary spirit which would later make her an ardent supporter of Fidel Castro by eloping to New York at the age of fifteen. There she received her Russian-based training at the Vilzak-Shollar School and the School of American Ballet and made her way into the fledgling Ballet Theatre. In early pictures she is very much the child bride—wide-apart sloe eyes and creamy skin, a combination of ingenuousness and sensuality that she would bring to her most famous role, Giselle.

Igor Youskevitch was born in Russia in the year the *Titanic* sank. Both Imperial Russia and the world of easy wealth epitomized by the liner were shattering, and at the time of the Russian Revolution Youskevitch's family fled to Yugoslavia. He was raised as a gentleman, with habits of courtliness so ingrained that they became as striking a part of his dance style as his technique. Writing of his "elegant and even

Giselle. Photo: Dance Collection, The New York Public Library at Lincoln Center

insinuating grace," Edwin Denby would observe "his courtesy and his modest charm;" and Ann Barzel said, "Youskevitch's simple style and excellent stage decorum are as aristocratic as ballet." Youskevitch came to ballet by the Olympian route of a talented athlete. He had awards in gymnastics, track, and swimming by the time he took up dancing. His coordination and the fact that he was used to doing his sports training to music helped him to make remarkable progress in his new discipline, and after only two months he was regularly partnering Yugoslavian ballerina Xenia Grunt. He also received some training in engineering and retained throughout his career a meticulous and scientific approach to performances. But he finally decided upon ballet and went to study in Paris, where his technique was perfected but his courtly manner reinforced by Olga Preobrazhenska— the gentlest of the grand old Maryinsky ballerinas. Youskevitch danced with the Ballets Russes de Paris, briefly with de Basil's Ballet Russe, and then followed Massine to the Ballet Russe de Monte Carlo as a principal. But Youskevitch, though magnificent, did not flourish as the mercurial Frederic Franklin did in Massine's ebullient, chaotic character ballets. Youskevitch's drama was subtly colored and deeply felt. At the Monte Carlo, Youskevitch was a foothill—at Ballet Theatre, and with Alonso, he became a peak.

Duration of partnership: 1946–60
Companies: Ballet Theatre, 1946–55; Ballet Alicia Alonso, Ballet Nacional de Cuba, 1948–59; Ballet Russe de Monte Carlo, 1955–59
Principal Ballets: *Giselle, Swan Lake, Theme and Variations*

"Black Swan" pas de deux. Photo: Maurice Seymour

Theme and Variations. Photo: Dance Collection,
The New York Public Library at Lincoln Center

Beatrice Siegel writes of them, in her book
Alicia Alonso: "They enriched each other's
gifts, illuminating ballets with new spirit and
elegance, lighting up the stages of Europe and
America with their virtuoso dancing and their
deeply shared romanticism. He was always the
Prince supreme to her Sleeping Beauty, Juliet,
Giselle, the Enchanted Swan." But Alonso and
Youskevitch's first performance together
certainly didn't give any hint of the sublime
conjunction to come. Youskevitch had seen
Alonso give a memorable and smoldering
performance as Ate in Antony Tudor's
Undertow, and when she was proposed as a
substitute for the ailing Nora Kaye in the "Black
Swan" pas de deux he was happy to have her.
But Alonso had never danced the demanding
piece before. This first attempt was a disaster,
and she swore she would never do it again.
Youskevitch coaxed her back to it, and the rest

is history. It became one of their triumphs.
Youskevitch remembers, "I had quite a time to
convince her that . . . she will be very nice in it
and that it's her role, and this and that. Well,
she agreed to try again . . . and how right I
was."

Even in this early failure were the seeds of a
remarkable success and a remarkable
understanding between two people. For here
were two dancers who were able to talk about
their work. And talk they did, about everything
from the smallest technical adjustment to the
widest possible meaning. They discovered a
common romanticism, a common feeling for
detail and nuance, and a common desire to
extend classical structures to the limits of their
expression. "Technical details were
discussed," says Youskevitch, "but not for the
sake of technique. We both knew and
understood each other's individual technical
needs, and often planned details to serve overall artistic goals." They were not content to go
their separate ways on the stage—because
their way lay together. "Of course mostly with
Alicia it was completely different because we
planned the performance together. Not just
'here are a few steps that we do together and
the rest we are separate.' We planned what
she was doing, what I was doing. We were
never separated really. You see, whatever she
tried, whatever she does by herself, it's still
spiritually connected to what I'm going to do."
Alonso says, "In many ways it was like having
a conversation. Two people are talking to each
other." The two were able to turn their
conversations off stage into conversations on
stage. Youskevitch recalls a fascinating
approach to that sensational old war horse the
"Black Swan" pas de deux. By now completely
secure technically in what had become a
staple of their repertory, the two dancers were
trying to find some way to extend the purely
exhibitionistic nature of the piece (it wasn't until
1955 that the two performed the full-length
ballet): "She goes piqué à la seconde, and the
partner comes to her and she bends into his
arm and straightens up. It's purely a dancing
step . . . you know. Now we were trying to do a
kind of conversation of some kind. Some kind
of rapport, so she would do exactly the same
steps only when she would open the arms,
they would indicate 'What do you want from
me?'" Their aim was "whatever the technical
step was, to make it a little more interesting." In
this case, Alonso and Youskevitch got
precisely the response they were looking for
when one critic wrote, "A fairly shabby virtuoso
turn conveyed something of meaning far
beyond the work involved."

Not every performance went as planned.
Alonso was an impulsive performer who would
occasionally do something completely
unexpected. When chided by Youskevitch she

Swan Lake. Photo: Dance Collection, The New York Public Library at Lincoln Center would exclaim, "Oh, let me dance. I don't want to think." Sometimes she would hold a balance too long and Youskevitch, the engineer, would nudge her off. Once, when the tempo in the "Black Swan" became particularly lively, the athlete in Youskevitch took over from the courtier. After several brisk lifts, Alonso complained that he was handling her "like a sack of potatoes." The image was so far from swanlike that they broke into fits of giggles and were just saved by the curtain. When Youskevitch recalled the early Ballet Theatre days as "all of us laughing, laughing," he may have been thinking of things like this.

The ballet upon which Alonso and Youskevitch lavished the most time and discussion was their greatest triumph, *Giselle.* First as performers and later, in Cuba, as producers, they went over every detail, trying to reveal the ballet's inner logic in its outward form. Youskevitch, for instance, always believed that the heroine should fall forward on the sword in the mad scene, because it was a medieval gesture. "I have always trouble with everyone I danced with, except Alicia Alonso because she somehow understood little things like that. . . . We would generally think of what and how the version could be done better and much more impressively and more understandably and more artistically."

A historical beat behind Markova and Dolin in their performances of *Giselle,* Alonso and Youskevitch imbued this most romantic of ballets with their own special charismatic warmth and elegance. Walter Terry described Alonso's unique mood: "Through her impeccable classicism glows a Latin warmth which, in turn, effuses the entire ballet with a rich range of dramatic colors." He continued, "Igor Youskevitch was splendid, injecting humor where humor was appropriate and coloring the rest of his enactment with varying

degrees of gallantry, tenderness, passion, and remorse . . . his pure danced passages were brilliantly realized." Youskevitch, who considers that to some extent "one deals with such assignments more as an actor rather than a dancer," believes that Alonso is "the most sincere interpreter" of *Giselle* he has seen. John Martin found them both "brilliant" and noted their "conviction," as well as how Youskevitch's tender manner enhanced Alonso's femininity. ("She was very feminine," recalls Youskevitch.) And many years later their performance provided the young John Prinz, who would be a Ballet Theatre star himself, with an unforgettable experience. "When I saw them dance I cried. They had such a beautiful thing together on the stage. You could see a real love between them. Even at that age, I felt all the little delicacies, the little betrayals. When Youskevitch crawled at the end of *Giselle,* he had tears in his eyes."

The rapport between partners must be physical as well as mental, and this was particularly important in Alicia Alonso's case because her brilliance had been hampered very early on by the threat of blindness. In the 1940s alone, she had three eye operations and sometimes moved about the stage in uncertain trajectories. With Youskevitch, who was so much attuned to her and so understanding, she had complete security. "He had the natural manner of a danseur noble," she says, and he recalls, "We felt the movement in the same kind of tempo, in the same speed, and so that helped a lot."

We can see evidence of this rapport in films and photographs. The two dancers are as swift and mutually reflexive as rubber bands and dance with crystalline purity. Alonso's knees seem almost to have a life of their own, beautifully articulate, and her feet, as Youskevitch points out, are also beautiful. Even in the most difficult sequences, Youskevitch seems poised, and we can see what Selma Jeanne Cohen called "the miracle of his coordination and the nobility and beauty of his bearing." In still photographs, the dancers seem etched, and Youskevitch's hollow face complements Alonso's riper one. He at once cherishes and challenges her. Their combination of what Walter Terry called "dash and grace" made them the perfect exponents of Balanchine's challenging *Theme and Variations,* in which they created the leading roles. It is at once an homage to the stately and elaborate classicism of Marius Petipa in the grand days of the Imperial Ballet, which came to full flower in the full-length Tchaikovsky ballets like *The Sleeping Beauty,* and a modern abstraction pushing the dancers to the limits of their technique. "For the premier danseur it offers one of the most exciting solo

variations in ballet," wrote Walter Terry. "It provides the ballerina with the opportunity to display her speed, her smoothness and her assured agility, and it encourages them to dance together in a manner designed to reveal the ballerina's line and the cavalier's gallant concern for both her loveliness and her balance." Balanchine thought Alonso and Youskevitch danced the adagio too romantically, but romance was second nature to them, and *Theme and Variations* does not seem to have suffered in its essence. "Alicia Alonso and Igor Youskevitch were magnificent throughout the ballet," Terry reported in a later review, "investing each movement, each phrase of action with knowing dynamic shadings, with technical accuracy, with aristocratic manner." "In dancing major abstract ballets," says Youskevitch, "one has to create a 'dance role.' The idea of the ballet, the rhythm and the character of the music, the type of choreographic dance steps all are the ingredients that generate ideas for a 'dance role.'" Alonso and Youskevitch added to *Theme and Variations*'s grand and buoyant structure an emotional logic all their own.

During the early 1950s, Alonso and Youskevitch were the mainstays of Ballet Theatre. Contracts were signed on the basis of their appearances, and they were widely acclaimed throughout America and Europe. They were the zenith of the company's 1953 European tour, charming London in *Giselle* and amazing Paris with the "Black Swan" pas de deux. At home, after the premiere of William Dollar's *Constantia,* in which they created leading roles, one critic wrote that they had entered the ranks of "the very great of the world of dance." "They had such perfection as a team, as if they were born to dance together," recalls old friend Maria Karnilova.

At the same time as their American triumphs, Alonso and Youskevitch were engaged in revitalizing ballet in Cuba. As early as 1948, during the temporary disbanding of Ballet Theatre, Alonso had formed Ballet Alicia Alonso with Youskevitch as partner and collaborator. They danced the complete *Swan Lake* for the first time, as well as Alberto Alonso's *Romeo and Juliet* and, of course, *Giselle,* which they staged together. They toured Cuba and then South America in hazardous conditions. Once, in a stadium so crowded the audience threatened to overflow the stage, an offensive member of the audience was disposed of by passing him hand over hand over the heads of the people and dumping him on the other side of a wall. Once they crossed a bridge so rickety they had to get out of the bus and walk it across, as if it were an elephant. In Caracas, they ran into a military coup and were briefly stranded.

Don Quixote pas de deux. Photo: Dance Collection, The New York Public Library at Lincoln Center

Throughout all these adventures, the two dancers were sustained by their discussions and analyses of performances and productions, which kept up their interest and incentive while on tour.

In 1955, Alonso and Youskevitch joined the Ballet Russe de Monte Carlo and also continued to dance in Cuba, where Alonso's company, recognized as a national force, was now called Ballet de Cuba. Reviewing them in a Monte Carlo performance of *Harlequinade*, Ed Brooks called them "the royally starring pair," and John Martin was struck anew by *Swan Lake:* "In the dignity of bearing, the imperiousness of gesture one found the queen, while in the yielding quality of her dancing with the prince and in the suggestion of quiet ecstasy one witnessed the woman. Igor Youskevitch danced the role of the Prince with his customary grace and gallantry and he gave a welcome suggestion of dramatic purpose to his rather shadowy role."

After the Cuban Revolution of 1959, Alonso's company became the Ballet Nacional de Cuba. She held open auditions, and Youskevitch was on her panel of judges. They toured Latin America with this reconstituted company, and the two of them also appeared in the open air in New York's Central Park, in one of the earliest Theater-in-the-Park series, dancing classical pas de deux. In 1960, they were guests with American Ballet Theatre for its twentieth anniversary gala, where they displayed the terrific and tender sides of their personalities by dancing first the *Don Quixote* pas de deux and then *Giselle.* In 1961, the United States broke off diplomatic relations with Cuba. Politics, which had occasionally in conversation come between the fiery idealist Alonso and the mellower and more conservative Youskevitch, were suddenly an insuperable barrier. It was the end of a partnership, the beginning of a legend.

In 1975, the State Department gave Alicia Alonso permission to appear again in the United States, and in 1980 she and Youskevitch met again on stage at American Ballet Theatre's fortieth Anniversary Gala. They performed the Act I mime scene from *Giselle,* and the audience could see echoes of the "real love" and "little delicacies" that had so moved John Prinz.

Alicia Alonso, delicate and steely, passionate and vulnerable, and Igor Youskevitch, ardent and courteous, elevated, through their dramatic classicism, ideals of femininity and masculinity into spiritual ideals of tenderness and strength. They felt with movement and moved with feeling; and the bond between them became a visible part of their performances. They were, as Youskevitch says, "never separated really."

Maria Tallchief & André Eglevsky

"I never really knew what dancing was before!"
—Maria Tallchief

"She had quality."
—André Eglevsky

A popular Greek myth tells the story of how Theseus, king of Greece, wooed and wedded Hippolyta, the powerful queen of the Amazons. This story made its way into Chaucer's *Canterbury Tales* and also into Shakespeare's *A Midsummer Night's Dream*. Hippolyta is a striking character in George Balanchine's ballet based on this play. We see her crossing the stage in great stag leaps, but she eventually lays aside her bow—if not her strength—to become Theseus's bride.

Clearly there is something irresistible about the idea of a king and an Amazon, and perhaps this accounts for the magical partnership between the glamorous virtuoso André Eglevsky and the indomitable Maria Tallchief, who reigned at the New York City Ballet for the best part of a decade.

Tallchief and Eglevsky were Paganinis of the ballet. Faster and stronger than most of their contemporaries, they were for this very reason often isolated in performance. Eglevsky was chastised by critics for being an ungallant partner, a "ballerina adversary," as Olga Maynard called him; and Tallchief, revered for her brilliance, was yet considered something of an implacable ice-maiden. It wasn't until these two formidable talents came together in 1951 at the New York City Ballet that they were able to reach the peak of their powers and temper virtuosity with grace. "These two danced in thrilling harmony," Olga Maynard recalls.

With the benefit of hindsight, we can see some amusing parallels in the two dancers' lives. Both had romantic backgrounds. Eglevsky, born in the year of the Russian Revolution, was the son of a White Russian Cossack who fled to Nice. Tallchief, born in Oklahoma eight years later, was an Indian

Harlequinade Pas de Deux. Photo: Dance Collection, The New York Public Library at Lincoln Center

princess, whose family name was Ki He Kah Stah Tsa. Both were child prodigies. Under the auspices of a foolish teacher, Maria was already performing on pointe at the age of five. Coincidentally, when Eglevsky began dance training in Nice, men's ballet slippers, obtainable only from Paris, were very hard to come by, and he too began in pointe shoes. He went on to train in England and France with Nicholas Legat, Alexander Volinine, and Olga Preobrazhenska. Fokine soon spotted this prodigious youth, and at fourteen Eglevsky was already starring in Colonel de Basil's Ballet Russe. One critic, pinpointing his combination

---

Duration of partnership: 1951–59, occasionally 1960s
Companies: New York City Ballet, 1951–59; Eglevsky Ballet, 1960s, concert groups
Principal Ballets: *À la Françaix, Capriccio Brillante, Harlequinade Pas de Deux, The Nutcracker, Pas de Trois* (Minkus), *Scotch Symphony, Swan Lake, Sylvia Pas de Deux*

Sylvia Pas De Deux. Photo: Courtesy Mrs. André Eglevsky

of spacious athleticism, warmth, and youthfulness, called him a "lion cub," and Edwin Denby would later refer to "that large open-heartedness that he alone brings to classic dancing." Eglevsky was in some ways a restless and temperamental man, and by the time he reached the New York City Ballet, he had been a premier danseur with every major Western company operating at the time. He danced a number of dramatic roles (he was, for instance, Alicia Alonso's first Albrecht), but Walter Terry, seeing him with the Ballet Russe de Monte Carlo, predicted that he would be better "as a protagonist of pure dance roles" of the kind he would find at City Ballet. During his time with the Ballet Russe de Monte Carlo, Eglevsky probably encountered the young Maria Tallchief, who joined the company at seventeen after studying with Bronislava

Swan Lake. Photo: Dance Collection, The New York Public Library at Lincoln Center

Nijinska. Two years later she was spotted by George Balanchine, who made her a ballerina and, briefly, his wife. By the time Eglevsky joined the New York City Ballet, Tallchief had already made her name as the chillingly seductive and compelling fairy in Balanchine's revival of *Le Baiser de la Fée* and most of all as the swift and electrifying heroine of his *Firebird.* Eglevsky was known everywhere for his "massive, heroic yet amazingly pliable physique," as Baird Hastings wrote in *Ballet Review,* for his effortless and endless pirouettes, and for his great catlike jump. It only remained to bring the two together.

André Eglevsky made his debut with the New York City Ballet on 17 February 1951, in Balanchine's *Sylvia Pas de Deux* with Tallchief. This elegant but fiendish piece became so much identified with the pair that it was hard to remember that it was originally created for another man. It was obvious to everyone that an exciting match had been made, and an exciting performance resulted. "The result," recalled Anatole Chujoy in his book on the company, "was an exciting exhibition by both dancers of technical virtuosity, élan, and brio not often seen on the ballet stage." Tallchief was set afire, as befitted a firebird, and, wrote John Martin, "André Eglevsky caught the contagion from the very beginning, as a sensitive partner should. There were moments when, with Maria Tallchief and André Eglevsky on stage, physical enchantment took on metaphysical values." This is a dancer's highest achievement—to make movements stand for something beyond themselves. *Sylvia* was bravura in the French manner. It required a wicked elegance to go with its hair-raising feats of virtuosity, and no one was more astonished than the dancers themselves. Though Tallchief and Eglevsky had danced the "Black Swan" pas de deux together on television, it was through the *Sylvia Pas de Deux* that they first came to realize each other's quality. "André was incredible," says Tallchief. "I don't know anyone else who could have done it. The steps, the partnering, the timing— turns, balances, promenades—it was a tour de force." Eglevsky remembered, "The girl's variation was exquisite. In the coda, Maria did a series of relevé turns en attitude en avant with arms closed at unbelievable speed— unbelievable—and clean, clean, clean."

In an interview with *Ballet Review* shortly before he died, Eglevsky said that he believed Balanchine "creates a dancer in choreography." Balanchine knew he had exceptional clay to work with in Tallchief and Eglevsky, and the early years of their partnership signaled a burst of creative energy from Balanchine. He was as fascinated as everyone else by their technique and seemed to be trying to test its limits, as though it were tempered steel. The Minkus *Pas de Trois,* with Nora Kaye and later Melissa Hayden, was light, fun, and fast and, according to Chujoy, "evoked a storm of applause." *Capriccio Brillante* was a kind of visual concert about turns, something its two principals could do without thinking. Chujoy admired their "élan, ease, and simplicity," and Walter Terry called it "sweet and neat." Balanchine made an ingenious bauble in *À la Françaix,* a tongue-in-chic ballet joke—*Giselle* at the U.S. Open—in which Eglevsky's spruce "Tennis anyone?" young man, busy breaking hearts on the courts, is wooed away by Tallchief's "supercilious Sylphide" (as Chujoy called her).

Eglevsky remembered that the first thing Balanchine said when Eglevsky joined the company was, "I have Maria and André and I can do, now, *Swan Lake.*" Toward the end of 1951 he realized this long-cherished ambition to produce his own version of the famous classic.

Balanchine's version of *Swan Lake* reduced a four-act ballet to one act, and most of the choreography was drastically altered, but the dramatic tension of the work remained the same. Eglevsky, as Prince Siegfried, encounters the magical Swan Queen and then loses her to the evil sorcerer Rothbart. (In this version there is no optimistic apotheosis.) The first few performances were not an unqualified success. Walter Terry wrote favorably of Tallchief's "royal bearing" and "grandeur of balletic line" and praised Eglevsky for gallantry and handsome dancing, but generally the consensus was that the atmosphere was chilly and remote without sufficient authority and pathos. However, great partnerships, like good marriages, expand and mature, and *Swan Lake* showed the first signs of this change in the partnership of Tallchief and Eglevsky. The subtle alchemy that makes great partnership was at work, and by 1952, critics were noting a new passionate warmth, especially in Tallchief, who revealed, according to Olga Maynard, "a serenity and radiance so palpable that it illuminated the stage." Of a later performance of *Swan Lake,* John Martin observed, "Maria Tallchief's performance of the chief role has grown miraculously. It has acquired a grandeur which it never had before; it is warm and womanly, keyed to a gracious dignity. . . . André Eglevsky managed the prince's tremendously difficult variation with stirring command. . . . [It was] an exceptionally alive and dramatically gracious realization of the role of the prince." Edwin Denby gives a moving account of the effect upon him of one of these emotionally enriched performances: "Tallchief's head positions were a sharp pleasure." And of the end: "Hundreds of birds beginning to take

Pas de Trois Classic (Minkus *Pas de Trois*). Photo: Dance Collection, The New York Public Library at Lincoln Center

off, swirling in the air all over the stage, a beating of wings as they rise up, these great birds at arms length—after they had gone and the toy swans were swimming back along the drop and Eglevsky looked at them immobile, and I looked with him . . . just then I realized with a miserable pang that she had been transformed back into a beast and that she was lost, lost forever. Lost to me too." Praise also resounded when the New York City Ballet showed *Swan Lake* on its European tour in 1952. Tallchief and Eglevsky received fifteen curtain calls from the usually phlegmatic Swiss. The ballet was also responsible for one of the rare quarrels in an exceptionally harmonious partnership. During one confusing rehearsal, in which Balanchine, that inveterate changer of steps, had yet again altered the adagio, Eglevsky turned where he was now expected to lift, and Tallchief fell flat on her face. He recalled tactfully, "She got up and looked back at me and was blunt."

Balanchine, who in some ways may have nurtured the changing performance style of his two stars, was certainly quick to exploit it in *Scotch Symphony,* a ballet which, with its yearning Scotsman and romantically distant sylph, was clearly modeled on *La Sylphide* and treated seriously themes the earlier *À la Françaix* had jested about. A perfect embodiment of Tallchief and Eglevsky's new radiant lyricism, *Scotch Symphony* was an immediate success. P. W. Manchester described it as "a most lovely and poetic conception, danced with the tenderest sensibility by Tallchief, who performs steps of the utmost difficulty without for a moment abandoning her new-found gentle radiance." Eglevsky was praised for his dancing and dramatic expressiveness, and Walter Terry described a magically harmonious moment between the two: "Tallchief flying through the air with gossamer lightness, sweetly rejecting gravity . . . when two boys toss Tallchief high in the air, she sails forward as if the air were her natural home, and Eglevsky catches her high on his chest as if she were without weight."

Tallchief and Eglevsky's new security and radiance was noticeable in everything they did, and even illuminated old favorites. Walter Terry wrote, "At the very start of the New York City Ballet's current season at City Center, Miss Tallchief made it quite clear that something new and wonderful had happened to her. Even the 'Sylvia' was aglow with warmth and touched by a softness . . . which in no way obscured the basic brilliance of the piece." John Martin noted in Eglevsky "a new graciousness and sense of pleasure in his performing." Of Tallchief he wrote, "Make no mistake, ballerina is not a title that can be bestowed by contract, it is a state that must be achieved." It is clear that Eglevsky helped Tallchief achieve it.

Now this incandescent pair was really launched as a partnership. Reviews became paeans: "Tallchief and Eglevsky . . . make your hair lift and your neck tingle." "Sometimes, watching them, you feel such ecstasy you can hardly bear it." "You haven't seen pas de deux danced until you've seen them!" Balanchine, ever finding new forms for them, made *Caracole* (with Patricia Wilde) and *Harlequinade Pas de Deux.*.*Caracole,* like its name, was fiendishly twisty and turning. "Flashing and brilliant," it reminded John Martin of *Theme and Variations.* "The variations for Tallchief and Wilde are breathtakingly rapid, rhythmic, and ingenious; that for Eglevsky may well be the most intricate passage ever created by Balanchine for a man." *Harlequinade Pas de Deux* was a mixed success. Walter Terry wrote, "As always, the two stars make a handsome pair, and they perform with that physical exactitude which is ever a joy to behold," but generally this distillation of the *commedia dell'arte* did not really suit the pair. They were better when their talents were elegantly adorned, spiced, but not consumed by character. It was not until the arrival of Patricia McBride and Edward Villella, for whom he also did a *Harlequinade,* that Balanchine would have a pair vigorous, flirtatious, and zany in quite the right way for this sort of piece. Balanchine also set the grand adagio in *The Nutcracker,* for the Sugar Plum Fairy and her cavalier, on Tallchief and Eglevsky, but injury prevented Eglevsky from dancing it on opening night.

It became, however, with the *Sylvia Pas de Deux,* the staple of the small concert tours Tallchief and Eglevsky began to do in the mid-1950s. At New York's Lewisohn Stadium, Judith Crist described the two pieces as "ideal vehicles for the two stars. With vivacity and style, they illustrate not only the beauties and techniques of classical ballet, but also their own special power and grace as masters of the form. Their color brought bravos and applause from the well-filled stadium, matched only by the enthusiastic response to their duets . . . Miss Tallchief and Eglevsky . . . provided the magic that brings from the audience a breathless hush and sudden applause." Another review, of a program given at the Eastman Theatre, was a tribute to the pair's special relationship in its maturity: "The two dancers . . . are perfect partners. Their dances together are models of rhythm and precise timing, and even in the acrobatic twirls and flings which seem to be inevitable features of a program of this sort, there were delightful grace, fluency, and delicacy of accent."

"It was my lovely, lovely period," Eglevsky recalled. "Maria was a lovely dancer, and we could have made a team like Margot and Rudi." As it was, the pair made a then-unprecedented $1,000 per guest performance, and this enabled Eglevsky to found his own school and company, where Tallchief would guest in the mid-1960s.

André Eglevsky gave his last performance with the New York City Ballet in 1959, ending, as he had begun, in the *Sylvia Pas de Deux* with Maria Tallchief. The partnership had come full circle—but it was a revolution filled with growth and weight. "I never really knew what dancing was before!" said Tallchief. "She was brilliant," returned Eglevsky. "She was a finished dancer. She had quality."

The dancers grew together, complemented and supported one another: her balance, his elevation, her cold fire, his gregarious devouring warmth. Their straight features could be implacable—with each other they seemed pure but human. They had much to give each other, but their partnership was given a special glow by the nurturing of George Balanchine. It was through him and his works that their talents were most fully realized. This is what Eglevsky meant when he said, "I think [Balanchine] creates a dancer in choreography." In an early essay called "Some Thoughts About Classicism and George Balanchine," Edwin Denby defined the Balanchinian ideals: "A gift for coherent, vigorous, positive, unsimpering movement, and a gift too for a powerful spontaneous rhythmic pulse in action." He might have been talking about Tallchief and Eglevsky.

Scotch Symphony. Photo: Courtesy Mrs. André Eglevsky

Melissa Hayden & Jacques d'Amboise

"Many of the greatest moments they have given over the years have been when they were together, dancing with that instinctive sensibility that informs all of ballet's finest partnerships."
—Clive Barnes

On 28 November 1969, Melissa Hayden and Jacques d'Amboise celebrated their twentieth anniversary with New York City Ballet. Clive Barnes wrote, "They have grown up together in the same company, and many of the greatest moments they have given over the years have been when they were together, dancing with that instinctive sensibility that informs all of ballet's finest partnerships." The pair danced Balanchine's Tchaikovsky *Pas de Deux,* a dazzling showpiece that they had given a special glow over the years, and Anna Kisselgoff commented on the special feeling in the theater. "Jacques d'Amboise gave Melissa Hayden a hug. Miss Hayden gave Mr. d'Amboise a hug. A sold-out house at the State Theatre gave both of them an ovation. Miss Hayden received a bouquet of chrysanthemums and Mr. d'Amboise got a wreath, which he slung over his shoulder like a French brigadier general." The performance seemed to catch fire. "From the moment the pair began this classical showpiece it was apparent that this was a special occasion. Their partnering spelled consideration for each other and excitement for the populace. Their variations brought out the best in each. Miss Hayden's technical assurance and breathtaking ballerina manner; Mr. d'Amboise's gallantry of style and masculine virtuosity . . . they were in exceptional form."

The Hayden-d'Amboise partnership was forged in the flame of George Balanchine's genius, and as his company grew, they grew with it. "Looking back at it," says Hayden, "I feel that at the time, when it first started, it may have been accidental, and then, since it worked for him visually, and we seemed to complement each other emotionally, we

Picnic at Tintagel. Photo: Dance Collection, The New York Public Library at Lincoln Center

sparked each other, and that in itself may have sparked Mr. Balanchine's imagination."

The two dancers came to Balanchine by different routes. Canadian-born Hayden had three seasons with Ballet Theatre (where Antony Tudor changed her name from Mildred Herman) from 1945 to 1948, and from there to two years of rather gypsyish life touring South America with the Ballet Alicia Alonso. It was during one of these tours, whose chaos would have made Eva Perón blink, that Hayden wrote to and was accepted by the fledgling City Ballet. She joined the company in 1950 when

---

Duration of partnership: 1954–73
Company: New York City Ballet
Principal Ballets: *Cortège Hongrois, The Figure in the Carpet, Medea, The Nutcracker, Raymonda Variations, Stars and Stripes, The Still Point, Swan Lake,* Tchaikovsky *Pas de Deux*

Tchaikovsky *Pas de Deux.* Photo: Martha Swope

Apollo. Photo: Fred Fehl

further two years with Ballet Theatre. She danced Iseult (following Diana Adams), and d'Amboise had his first big role as Tristan.

D'Amboise was already developing the winning manner that would endear him to so many audiences over the years, an unquenchable exuberance Hayden calls "the extrovert quality that he added to the choreography." Hayden, on the other hand, was an introvert, but one whose passionate absorption in her material blazed across the footlights and amounted to a form of bravura in itself. "People said I came on stage and the stage lit up," recalls Hayden. "I don't think I came on with that intention. I think my presence might have been imposing for some people only because I was *that* involved in what I was doing." Balanchine cast them in the technically dazzling *Pas de Dix* (originally made on Maria Tallchief and André Eglevsky), where their combined styles made an immediate impact. "If in *Pas de Dix,* Miss Hayden approached the fabulous," wrote Walter Terry, "so also did Jacques d'Amboise as her partner. The young premier danseur gave us the best of his floating leaps, his easy aerial beats, his faultless spin, in addition to an ingratiating presence." Nearly twenty years later Balanchine would adapt this music and the ballerina's regal and faintly Oriental solo for *Cortège Hongrois,* his homage and present to Hayden on her retirement. D'Amboise had not long before returned from Hollywood, where he had been testing his ingratiating presence before a wider audience. Among the films he appeared in was *Seven Brides for Seven Brothers.* In their book, *Danseur: The Male in Ballet,* Richard Philp and Mary Whitney write that d'Amboise "helped to shape a new image of the danseur as an all-American boy," and one of the first roles he had on his return to City Ballet in 1956 was an embodiment of this ideal. The ballet was Todd Bolender's *The Still Point,* a delicate piece about youthful loneliness and first love, and it consolidated the Hayden-d'Amboise partnership. The work had been done originally for a small troupe, including non-dancers, and it was a measure of Hayden's and d'Amboise's skill that they managed to translate it to the ballet stage without destroying its simplicity. Bolender says, "I visualized it as a dialogue between the two, really as though they were speaking to each other—not dancing, but speaking." In their roles as a young girl shunned by her companions and the boy with whom she discovers love, Hayden and d'Amboise were able to convey this almost "conversational" intimacy. Doris Hering reported: "Hayden wove endless nuance and pathos into her portrayal, and yet the danced outlines were contained and beautifully clear. D'Amboise

d'Amboise was still in the School of American Ballet. (She, whose training was so varied, would later say she admired d'Amboise's pure single schooling.) He may have had a chance to admire her at work in John Cranko's *The Witch,* where she played a possessed peasant girl and he is listed flatteringly as one of two "Bald Heads."

Oddly, Hayden and d'Amboise first really appeared together, not in a Balanchine ballet, but in Sir Frederick Ashton's *Picnic at Tintagel,* in which a group of travelers in Cornwall find themselves reenacting the legend of Tristan and Iseult. It was 1954, and Hayden had just returned to the New York City Ballet after a communicated the steady masculinity that we have associated heretofore only with Youskevitch." Both dancers were praised for their dramatic ability. Walter Terry called Hayden an "actress-dancer" and noted "a fine characterization by Jacques d'Amboise as the young man. His gentle firmness and continuing devotion were beautifully matched with the volatile actions of the girl." P. W. Manchester concurred: "Here he [d'Amboise] emerges as a fine, serious artist and an admirable partner in the great pas de deux which is the long, splendid climax of a work which is romantic, lyrical and deeply poignant." Of *The Still Point* Hayden said, "My whole body was to express my feelings." Some years later in a book of ballet stories intended for children, she outlined the plot of *The Still Point* as a story about growing up, and called the young man in it Jacques.

Happy in this winning combination, Bolender made *The Masquers* on the pair the following year. The story of a selfless young woman betrayed by an arrogant soldier did not prove to be very interesting or successful, but Hayden and d'Amboise were praised for making the best they could out of stock characters and a stock situation.

In *Picnic at Tintagel,* Hayden and d'Amboise played relatively modern characters, touched for a moment by myth. In Birgit Cullberg's *Medea* they were asked to bring the myth itself to life. Again, reviews were mixed, but again there was great praise for the stars' ability to bring drama to life through dancing. John Martin complimented Hayden on a "richly colored . . . dramatic characterization," and d'Amboise for "dancing miraculously [and] channeling a firm and consistent dramatic stream through his technical skill as a dancer." Hayden's passionate nature, which usually shimmered beneath the surface of Balanchine's neoclassical ballets, was here let loose in tooth and claw. Walter Terry wrote of her Medea: "A portrayal which squeezed every ounce of drama and melodrama, passion and poignancy, out of a vivid and terrifying role. Not only was Hayden the superb actress here but also a glittering dance technician who stirred the viewer with her physical skill as well as with her dramatic powers."

George Balanchine, in his ballets, distilled his dancers' dramatic qualities and technical facility to their essence. Hayden, with what one critic summarized as her "suppleness, lyricism, bravura, ferocity, sense of comedy, fabulous technical facility," and d'Amboise, with his free and powerful style and charm of manner, often became the crown of Balanchine's choreographic images. Hayden says, "There were certain ballets Mr. Balanchine saw us in— they were romantic, dramatic." Perhaps nothing

Stars and Stripes. Photo: Martha Swope

demonstrates this so well as their exuberant Liberty Bell and El Capitan pas de deux in *Stars and Stripes,* done in the same year as *Medea.* It was the crisp center of this ever-popular ballet-military extravaganza. As Nancy Reynolds describes it, "An all-American boy, grinning from ear to ear, meets a sweet girl who eyes him tenderly, then lays her head on his shoulder . . . Together they bring down the house with some more-than-energetic dancing—splits, jumps, lifts, multiple turns in a circle for the lady, double bent-knee air turns for her soldier and then she is carried off, with a longing backward glance, resting daintily on his chest." This carefree bravura, with Hayden as d'Amboise's pert and seductive Yankee Doodle Dandy, brought the house down. Walter Terry wrote, "His pompous General Grant stance and her steely imperiousness were bright bits of flavor in spectacular dancing," and P. W. Manchester recorded, "They piled climax upon climax until the audience was in a state of almost gibbering excitement." From the basic material of the choreography, Hayden and d'Amboise built a comic vignette. "Jacques began to add funny bits," Hayden recalled, a pattern that reflected their working relationship, both in the company and on the many concert tours and lecture demonstrations. "I always felt I was his straight man," says Hayden. "I was the straight comic, and he was very exuberant. For me, he was always a big splash of color, and I guess I added a texture."

Color and texture were, in fact, the two elements of the next work Balanchine made on them. *The Figure in the Carpet* told the story of Persia through the metaphor of carpet-weaving, massing extravagant images from the sterile desert to the building of Paradise. Hayden and d'Amboise, as the Prince and Princess of Persia, were the apotheosis of that Eden. They posed cool and regal, before a gushing fountain, before their long and intricate pas de deux. "Comporting themselves with grandeur," as Walter Terry wrote, "and a touch of hauteur . . . their pas de deux was a beauty and they danced it handsomely." P. W. Manchester said simply, "The Persian dream was fulfilled." Other roles with a similar grandeur included the lead couple in *Raymonda Variations* (the female lead was danced originally by Patricia Wilde but was probably intended for Hayden until she became pregnant), a distillation of Balanchine's stylistic heritage from Marius Petipa, and of 19th-century Russian sumptuousness, and the "Divertissement" pas de deux in *A Midsummer Night's Dream.* The ballerina's solos in *Raymonda,* described by another dancer as being both "lyrical and brilliant," suited Hayden's combination of dash and drama. In *A Midsummer Night's Dream*

Hayden was originally cast as Titania. When she began to dance the divertissement with d'Amboise, she brought to it the same regality, softened by her special rapport with her partner. This was certainly one of the "romantic, dramatic" things in which Balanchine liked to see them. In a ballet about the frailties of all sorts of love, human and divine, it is the one perfect image of a consummated emotion, and is at once a bravura set piece and an intimate moment. The pair also danced the pas de deux from *The Nutcracker* and a wide range of roles that reflected what Hayden calls their "multifaceted temperament." When d'Amboise created his own light, romantic *Irish Fantasy* in 1964, he cast Hayden in the lead. He himself tried the challenging role of Apollo, the raw young god who is tamed by art, and became the greatest interpreter of his generation. Hayden was one of his attendant muses. Hayden had long coveted the role of the Swan Queen in *Swan Lake,* but the role was never assigned her. She finally got her chance, at a moment's notice, when another dancer became ill on an Australian tour, and, of course, she asked for d'Amboise to support her. ("He was like a brother," says Hayden.) The ballet became one of their successes. Glenna Syse reviewed a later performance in Chicago. "Miss Hayden is a swan rejoicing in the transition from feather and down to flesh and blood. And I can't remember her dancing better. The legs are devastating, the arms liquid fire. And d'Amboise is a matchless partner, catching the special sense of the interpretation with bold ardor and the handsomest of styles." Balanchine's *Swan Lake,* though the same as the full-length original in emotional tone, is a shortened and rechoreographed version of the white acts. Hayden and d'Amboise got their chance to dance a more conventional classic when they were invited to do *Giselle* with Ballet West. Hayden had been brought up with the Alicia Alonso-Igor Youskevitch performance at Ballet Theatre, and was able to guide d'Amboise. "It was very exciting . . . a learning experience all the way around," she recalls.

"Very exciting" sums up the Hayden-d'Amboise partnership. It had a dynamic, new-minted quality about it, stemming from the pair's working relationship. "Two people have to respond to each other in a working relationship," says Hayden. "You need to have empathy, focus, and a goal. It's not just working with each other, it's working through things you specifically want to accomplish, not just the technical aspects of a relationship, but the artistic. His personality excited me. Many times you could rehearse a ballet, and prepare with Jacques, and then we got on stage, and he never did anything from rehearsal—

Cortège Hongrois. Photo: Martha Swope

physically we did, but the mood was sparked by our own response to each other, to the music and the situation." This interaction and spontaneity were noted by one reviewer who saw them in concert, "each challenging the other's best into a most stimulating partnership." "They are ingratiating performers. Audiences cherish them."

It is notable that one of the greatest successes of their partnership should be Balanchine's Tchaikovsky *Pas de Deux.* This bravura showpiece is pure dance, and any nuance comes from the performers themselves. With Hayden and d'Amboise courtliness stepped into the modern age. His grin, her uplifted chin, their vitality, made it live. "In the Tchaikovsky, Melissa Hayden and Jacques d'Amboise gave another master lesson in how

to remember more than most dancers forget," wrote Joseph Gale. And Saul Goodman had the key: "Obviously, they enjoyed dancing together."

In 1973 Melissa Hayden retired from New York City Ballet and from dancing. For her farewell, and his farewell to her, George Balanchine created *Cortège Hongrois.* To the Glazunov music for *Raymonda,* the piece captured the spirit of Imperial Russia, for a ballerina who had become truly imperial. Hayden's cavalier was, of course, d'Amboise, and her solo was taken from *Pas de Dix,* one of the first ballets they danced together. In the photographs of the finale to *Cortège* we can see them, standing before the corps, arms outflung, poised, confident, glittering, the grand image of a great partnership.

Margot Fonteyn & Rudolf Nureyev

Giselle and Albrecht, Odette and Siegfried, Aurora and Florimund, Romeo and Juliet, Marguerite and Armand, Pelleas and Melisande, Adam and Eve. No partnership in the history of ballet has epitomized so many lovers for so many as that of Margot Fonteyn and Rudolf Nureyev. And what could be more romantic in itself than the conjunction of these two stars—the cool, regal English ballerina, the reigning queen of her profession, and the volatile, tempestuous Tartar at the very beginning of a dazzling career? They showed the world a combination of air and fire such as it had not seen since Nijinsky leaped through Karsavina's window in *Le Spectre de la Rose,* fifty years before.

Fonteyn, cherished and encouraged by her parents, went from a prosperous and secure family environment into the fledgling Vic-Wells Ballet. Nurtured by the indomitable and far-seeing Ninette de Valois, she soon became its leading ballerina, went on serenely from triumph to triumph, and gained, over the years, the affection and respect of half the world.

In the other half, in the year in which she first did *Swan Lake,* Rudolf Nureyev was born into conditions of extreme hardship. Although his dancing was not encouraged, it was an unquenchable impulse in him, and he eventually found his way to the Kirov School, where he was accepted with these daunting cautionary words: "Young man, you will either become a brilliant dancer or a total failure—and most likely you'll be a failure." (Nureyev fans cherish this remark gleefully, and one is reminded of the possibly apocryphal transcription of Fred Astaire's first screen test: "Can't act. Balding. Can dance a little.")

The two halves of the partnership came together not long after Nureyev's famous leap of freedom to the West, when Fonteyn invited him to appear at one of her annual Royal Academy of Dancing (RAD) galas. She had first tracked him down at the Copenhagen apartment of her old teacher Vera Volkova. Volkova, enthusiastic, reported that she knew Nureyev was a genius—he had "the nostrils."

Fonteyn arranged to meet "the nostrils" by smuggling them into London under an assumed name. Nureyev turned up at her flat, pinched and wary, and she gave him tea. "I said something light and silly," Fonteyn writes. "Suddenly he laughed and his whole face changed. He lost the 'on guard' look, and his smile was generous and captivating. 'Oh, thank goodness!' I said. 'I didn't know Russians laughed.'" Nureyev had no doubts after this first meeting. "From the first moment I knew I had found a friend." Although Fonteyn did not dance with Nureyev at the RAD gala, she was enormously impressed by the passion and abandon with which he performed. When Ninette de Valois offered her the chance to dance *Giselle* with him in three months time, Fonteyn conquered her misgivings about "mutton dancing with lamb" and accepted.

Their first rehearsals gave some hint of what was to come. Fonteyn recalls, "Two hours passed in no time at all. I was Giselle and he Albrecht. He literally became Albrecht, and there was an extraordinary harmony between our interpretations." We see here a hint of the conviction and absorption in one another that was to make them unique. Even so unschooled an observer as Gloria Steinem was to write, "Fonteyn and Nureyev make us watch their life stories with rapt attention, for they may never happen again."

On 21 February 1962, before a full house feverish with anticipation, the pair gave an unforgettable performance of *Giselle.* At the end, Fonteyn plucked a long-stemmed rose from her bouquet and handed it to Nureyev, who sank on one knee and kissed her hand. The gesture was a theatrical convention, but never had it seemed to say—and promise—more. Covent Garden roared through twenty-three curtain calls, and a legend was born. "It was his way," Fonteyn sensitively observes, "of expressing genuine feelings, untainted by conventional words. Thereafter, a strange attachment formed between us which we have never been able to explain satisfactorily, and which, in a way, one could describe as a deep affection or love."

The performance dropped a pebble in the pond of the public which would ripple for

---

Duration of partnership: 1962–77
Companies: The Royal Ballet, Nureyev and Friends, guest appearances with numerous companies throughout the world
Principal Ballets: *Corsaire, Gayané, Giselle, Marguerite and Armand, Paradise Lost, Pelleas and Melisande, Romeo and Juliet, The Sleeping Beauty, Swan Lake*

Marguerite and Armand

twenty years, but it was left to the critics to analyze exactly what had happened. Richard Buckle wrote, "We have come to think of ballet partnerships as being made in the classroom and on the stage over the years of patient working together, but on Wednesday, we learned that they are made in heaven." "There was no break in the current of acting and moving, no switch from one idiom to another," recalls Alexander Bland. "It was a finely nuanced performance which preserved a fresh sense of spontaneity." He described the partnership as a kind of celestial accident. When the pair first appeared in New York in *Giselle,* Walter Terry agreed. "In this *Giselle* . . . one should not take Fonteyn and Nureyev separately. Each retains an identity, of course, but together they make a magic. They move, in simplest gesture or through actions which carry them into space, as one. The world of ballet has seen nothing quite like it in our time."

The next test of the new collaboration was *Swan Lake,* and it showed how much their instinctive rapport could triumph over technical difficulties. Rehearsals were full of seemingly unresolvable conflicts about staging and interpretation, but actual performances showed only a profoundly moving continuity of feeling. Alexander Bland writes, in *Fonteyn and Nureyev,* "The understanding between the two dancers seemed to reach a peak in this ballet. The smallest nuance of movement evoked an answering response. The dancing poured from them in an unbroken stream leaving at the end a sense of loss as though something unrecapturable had gone." As Nureyev himself remarked, "When I dance with Margot, it is one aim, there is one vision. It is painful arriving at that vision, but when we have found it, we go there together. There is no tearing us apart."

At first, people were most struck by how Nureyev affected Fonteyn. When Lincoln Kirstein first saw her dance, he found her "wonderful but unawakened." Nureyev's seemed to be the kiss that finally woke this sleeping beauty to her full potential. In a 1963 article prophetically entitled "The Hottest Little Team in Show Biz," Walter Terry wrote, "The sparks that Nureyev struck have set her aglow with a new-found grace and beauty." Siriol Hugh-Jones agreed. "What the partnership seems to have provided for her is some sort of challenge—to dance at a higher pitch, modify and change interpretations we have come to know well over the years, develop some quality to match the climate of tremendous drama and physical excitement Nureyev generates." "Margot Fonteyn, inspired and excited by her new partner, Rudolf Nureyev, gave some of the greatest performances of her career," reported Mary Clarke and Clement Crisp in *Ballet Annual.* Nureyev introduced Fonteyn to new

works, like the sprightly "Kurdish" pas de deux from *Gayané,* in which she seemed to look with impish wonder on his devouring leaps, and the unforgettable *Le Corsaire,* which has become one of the fixed symbols of their partnership. "A splendid vehicle for displaying his panther-like softness and exoticism, it paradoxically showed Fonteyn at her most chic, precise and elegant. The outrageous blending of the two quite different schools and styles succeeded brilliantly," wrote Clarke and Crisp. It became more and more apparent that the special magic of this partnership lay not merely in Nureyev's challenge to Fonteyn, but in the way their two styles blended. Beneath Fonteyn's cool classicism was a warmth and femininity that had made her probably the most beloved ballerina in history—Nureyev brought it to the surface and to the highest pitch of dramatic intensity. He was all fire and impulse on the surface, but capable of intense concentration and discipline. In Fonteyn he found someone to channel his ardor. "Each served as a foil for the other's dancing temperament, Fonteyn's sweet radiance and classical style complementing Nureyev's turbulent physicality," observed Tobi Tobias. But "it was paradoxical," Fonteyn writes, "that the young boy everyone thought so wild and spontaneous in his dancing cared desperately about

Giselle. Photo: Zoë Dominic

Gayané. Photo: Zoë Dominic

technique, whereas I, the cool English ballerina, was so much more interested in the emotional aspect of the performance." What they shared was overwhelming conviction as theatrical artists, an absorption in their characters and the emotions between them that made each moment seem uniquely passionate, irreplaceable—almost private. In a performance of *Les Sylphides, The Times* reported that they were "caught up in the same music, borne along on the same stream," and John Percival reports that the same paper's dramatic critic, Charles Lewsen, "told me that he had seen this pair only once, and what impressed him above all was the way their eyes seemed hardly ever to leave each other, maintaining a contact which ran between them like an electric current." As Nureyev put it, "Because we are sincere and gifted, an intense abstract love is born between us every time we dance together."

Their physical appearance enhanced their theatrical impact. On stage they appeared to be the highest form of two very different types of beauty. Fonteyn, with dark hair, dark eyes, and alabaster skin, could show every expression from celestial gravity to girlish excitement. She also had a perfectly proportioned slender body. Nureyev's muscles coiled under the skin like one of the wildcats to which he was often compared. He had a sensual proud face and a halo of golden hair worn sensationally long.

Fonteyn and Nureyev's theatrical intensity made them protean dancers—they could do almost anything, and as the partnership gained momentum, they did. In addition to *Giselle* and *Swan Lake,* they were cast in *Birthday Offering, Hamlet, Symphonic Variations,* and *Les*

Sylphides at the Royal Ballet. Fonteyn danced in Nureyev's early full-length ballet productions for other companies—*Swan Lake, Raymonda,* and *Sleeping Beauty*—and in his first staging in the West, the "Kingdom of the Shades" act from *La Bayadère* for the Royal Ballet. "At the center Fonteyn and Nureyev shone like stars from the east: her radiance and delicate line contrasted dazzlingly with his turbanned Oriental glamour," writes Alexander Bland. Inevitably, choreographers wanted to explore the potentials of this special partnership.

The first and greatest of the pieces done for them was Sir Frederick Ashton's *Marguerite and Armand,* based on the famous Alexandre Dumas novel about a dying courtesan, *La Dame aux Camélias.* It was an idea Ashton had been considering for years, and suddenly all the elements were at hand. "Quite by accident I heard this sonata of Liszt's one day on the wireless, and I sat there, and I saw the whole thing could be contained in this music. Margot seemed to me the epitome of Marguerite Gautier, and Rudolf seemed to me the epitome of Armand." Anticipation generated enormous excitement in the public for this emotional swashbuckler. Nureyev *was* Armand—ardent, passionate, extreme in love and in anger—and Fonteyn gave to the limits of her abilities as the beautiful, doomed Marguerite. Fonteyn describes a rehearsal in which, after she had run through the renunciation scene with Michael Somes as Armand's father, theatrical convention burst its bonds and real life came rushing in. "We came to the end and Rudolf tore into his entrance and the following pas de deux with a passion more real than life itself, generating one of those fantastic moments when a rehearsal becomes a burning performance." The actual performances, when they came, swept the audience away. "The most romantic duo in ballet today," exulted Walter Terry. Richard Buckle remembered the piece as a series of burning images. "The falling-in-love is wonderful. Nureyev with yearning arms is seen from behind, and as Fonteyn stands motionless, everything happens on her face. . . . I recall her bourréeing off, broken by duty and coughing; Nureyev's snakelike rage, his pointing at her in jeering love-hatred; her climbing into the air over his head to clutch at happiness, life and the sun before falling dead." He was moved to a kind of poetry: "To her deathbed, cloak swooping, a desperate nightrider, he soars." In the first great pas de deux, with Fonteyn bent backward in Nureyev's arms, her long tulle skirt about her like a fan, their clasped hands joined over her breast, they are the ultimate fulfillment of Blake's line about the "lineaments of gratified desire." Ashton said simply, "Together in my ballet they create an air of great love."

David Vaughan and Peter Brook were both struck by the way they moved beyond the confines of the ballet to create something so human it was almost holy. Vaughan wrote, "The final pas de deux has a kind of raw passion and desperation that are so real that one is almost embarrassed to watch." Director Peter Brook wrote, "When she and Nureyev stood together, tired and tender, a truly moving quality was experienced; they manifested to that audience a relationship grave, paler and less fleshbound than those of everyday life." *Marguerite and Armand* was unquestionably a vehicle for Fonteyn and Nureyev, but as Ashton pointed out, "There's nothing wrong with a vehicle provided it goes." It went.

Kenneth MacMillan made the poignant and sensuous *Divertimento* for the pair to dance at the Bath Music Festival of 1964. Just before the premiere, Fonteyn received word that her husband, Roberto Arias, had been shot in Panama. She very courageously went on to dance, and *Divertimento*'s single performance had a lingering poignancy for anyone who knew what pressure she was under. She and Nureyev triumphed again. "It was the complete entity of the two which drew magic out of the mime and music," reported the *Bath Weekly Chronicle.*

Shortly after the premiere of *Marguerite and Armand,* the pair made their New York debut with the Royal Ballet. Audiences, fed by rumors, were clamoring to see them, and this season began the evolution of Fonteyn and Nureyev into "Rudi and Margot," helped by reviews like this of Walter Terry's: "Combine the smolder, the mystery, the dynamic presence, the great streaks of vivid movement which Nureyev gives us with the beauty, the radiance, the womanliness, the queenliness, and the shining movement of Dame Margot and the cheers that have shaken the old Met to its foundations are explained . . . This, while Fonteyn and Nureyev were representing the most ephemeral, the most fleeting of all the arts, *was* ballet itself."

Soon the fans became as fascinated by "Rudi and Margot" offstage as on. Their smallest actions, especially together, were avidly reported and devoured, and they good-naturedly fended off rumors that their close friendship was more than that. As an example of more candid reporting, one photo caption read, "After their pas de deux, 'le twist' at the Sheraton-Palace." Nureyev, with his long hair and outlandish dress sense (including a snakeskin suit) was avidly drinking in all the entertainment the West had to offer, and Fonteyn, who had assisted her husband in a political coup and was once unsurprised to find a crate of grenades in her cellar, had a terrific sense of adventure. In 1967, they "set the

ballet world on its ear" when they were arrested on a drug charge at a party in Haight-Ashbury, San Francisco's hippie haven. The two are, of course, devout nonsmokers, and charges were dismissed. Audiences took them to their hearts and unfurled banners at the theater reading, "We love Rudi and Margot." So did nations. They danced at the White House for President Johnson, and the Austrian government issued a commemorative stamp when they did *Swan Lake* in Vienna. The list of countries at their feet is bounded only by the map.

Marguerite and Armand was made especially for Fonteyn and Nureyev and was tailored as the perfect medium for their gifts, but Kenneth MacMillan's *Romeo and Juliet,* for which they are equally well remembered, was created with two very different dancers in mind, and demonstrates how well the pair could transform any choreography and make it their own. Fonteyn brought all of her quality of what one critic called "suppressed ecstasy" to the role of Juliet, and the part of Romeo, originally rather dreamy and passive, came to life as buoyant and mischievous—passionate temperament and passionate dancing keeping apace. Never has Shakespeare's statement, "These violent delights have violent ends," been more fully realized than by this pair of lovers who never spoke the words. "There is an extraordinary moment at the end of the garden scene," reported Richard Buckle, "when she and Nureyev suddenly gaze horror struck at each other, thinking 'God! what agony love is!' . . . Fonteyn and Nureyev are incomparable for the luminosity of their personalities."

The ballet ended with forty-three curtain calls. The audience would not go home. In New York they had the same rapturous reception. "The kind of perfection in movement that they achieve together epitomizes the freedom that lies beyond technical mastery. It expresses

Romeo and Juliet. Photo: MIRA

Paradise Lost.

itself as poetic lyricism," reported the *New York Journal.* Fonteyn and Nureyev had found the heart of this best-loved of all romances.

The pair's venturesome spirit led them not only into the wilds of Haight-Ashbury, but into experiments in modern ballet and dance. One of their most successful collaborations was Roland Petit's lavishly outrageous Pop Art story of Adam and Eve, *Paradise Lost.* It was at once coolly and fiendishly athletic, while requiring the maximum in raw feeling, and they were king and queen of this not-so-innocent Eden. Richard Buckle was dazzled by their dramatic force: "Fonteyn's Eve had an amazing directness of drive and drama. Nureyev's Adam was ablaze with energy and life." The *Financial Times* concurred: "Adam is a tremendous role, one that magnificently exploits all the power, grace and emotion of Nureyev's dancing and one that he dances magnificently . . . Fonteyn has possibly not since *Symphonic Variations* had so exposed a part composed for her; and she is amazing. She looks and moves like a young girl. Every movement is expressive, compelling, revelatory." Fonteyn's own memoirs of the ballet are more personal and hilarious. She had to reach the stage by creeping along a 30-foot passage to reach a trap door, and recalls, "I was crawling along one particular night saying to myself 'This is a hell of a way to spend your forty-eighth birthday.'" She calls Nureyev's famous leap through a pair of gigantic lips "the kind of thing that really only happens in French ballets." Petit's next work for them, *Pelleas and Melisande,* was not-very-imaginative romantic slush, but everyone agreed they were lovely to look at. They found a greater challenge in being the first of ballet's ambassadors to modern dance when Martha Graham created *Lucifer* for them, with Nureyev in the title role and Fonteyn as a seductive Night. Arlene Croce commented on Nureyev's "magic aura of freedom" and "personal magnetism" and on Fonteyn's dramatic richness.

Fonteyn and Nureyev gave their last sustained performances together in 1977, when they appeared in *Les Sylphides* and *Marguerite and Armand* in London. A generation has grown up in their shadow, and they started a fire of enthusiasm that is still glowing today. It is as hard now as it was twenty years ago to analyze their special magic. "A kind of touchstone of togetherness has been set up," writes Alexander Bland, "by which other collaborations must be judged." John Gruen touched on the almost moral quality about the beauty of their dancing when he wrote, "Their appearances together are charged with almost overwhelming passion, nobility and symmetry," and Richard Philp and Mary Whitney speak of "a passionate solicitude that hinted at a visceral rapport beyond words." "Passion" and "electricity" were the words on every tongue.

The highest technique and dramatic ability combined with a singleness of vision and an emotional bond of such believability that the human heart shone beneath even the most elaborate trappings. As Peter Brook wrote, "All great art eventually is realistic; the art of these two dancers leads them continually to moments of truth."

Carla Fracci & Erik Bruhn

"To dance with Carla was to have fulfilled a love affair—a love affair consummated on the stage."
—Erik Bruhn
"We looked, we danced and loved . . . it was such a revelation and special partnership."
—Carla Fracci

"We looked, we danced—and loved," said Carla Fracci of her partnership with Erik Bruhn. And he agreed. "Having danced with Carla was like the fulfillment of a love affair—a love affair that was consummated on the stage." Great partnerships are always at work to give substance to the stuff of fairy tales. Fracci and Bruhn seemed to feel that their whole partnership was a fairy tale in itself, and this gave their work together its special sincerity and glow.

In these two dancers, two of ballet's romantic ideals met. Erik Bruhn was the ultimate prince: blond, aristocratic, impeccable, and aloof, but with a hint of passion beneath the imposing calm. (As another Danish dancer, Peter Martins, has said, "We Danes may seem very cool on the surface, but inside we're like a volcano.") Fracci, on the other hand, has always been the incarnation of the Romantic spirit, harking back to those great early Italian ballerinas Marie Taglioni, Carlotta Grisi, and Fanny Cerrito. Like them, her greatest roles would be the otherworldly Sylphide and Giselle, and like them, she has a vivid dark beauty, an air of great warmth and sweetness, and an uncanny lightness that makes the rise onto pointe seem just a finishing touch to a natural buoyancy. The pair seemed to have been drawn by a master draughtsman, and when describing them, people often thought in terms of art. "Miss Fracci . . . was like a romantic lithograph come to life," wrote Clive Barnes, and Mikhail Baryshnikov said of Bruhn, "It was as if he was a new type—like the perfect lithograph, but *real*. He was like an Ingres drawing—so fine, but so strong."

By a curious coincidence, Bruhn and Fracci were fostered by separate halves of another great romantic partnership, that of Alicia Markova and Anton Dolin. Bruhn, a child prodigy, was admired in Denmark almost from

his first steps, but international renown, even after several seasons with Ballet Theatre, was slow in coming. Bruhn was finally rocketed into prominence in 1955, when he made his debut in *Giselle* opposite Alicia Markova. From the moment he appeared on the stage, it was clear that this was going to be one of the great Albrechts in the history of the role, and the rapport between the two dancers was extraordinary. The performance was called "The Matinee that Made History." It would be nearly ten years before this Albrecht would find, again, a perfect Giselle in Carla Fracci.

Unlike Bruhn, Fracci was not hailed as a promising child. Underweight and frail, she was more like the runt who turned champion, or the ugly duckling who became a swan. Fracci's interest in ballet was transformed into a burning love after she saw Margot Fonteyn in *The Sleeping Beauty* when the Royal Ballet performed at La Scala. Her first big chance came when she persuaded the management to let her substitute for an injured dancer in Alfred Rodrigues's full-length *Cenerentola (Cinderella),* and her second when Anton Dolin asked her to perform at the Festival of Nervi. Dolin, like so many others after him, was struck by Fracci's romantic qualities, particularly by her resemblance to Fanny Cerrito, and invited her to take Cerrito's part in his staging of *Le Pas de Quatre.*

Among the impressed spectators at Nervi was Erik Bruhn, and when a friend who had seen Fracci dance at La Scala suggested that Bruhn introduce her to America, he agreed eagerly.

Carla Fracci and Erik Bruhn first appeared together in October of 1962. They danced excerpts, chosen by Bruhn, from *La Sylphide,* and Fracci remembers the experience as one of instant sympathy. "My English was practically non-existent. But we did not have to speak. It was an amazing thing, because it seemed as though we had known each other forever. Things functioned perfectly from the outset. It was like love-at-first-sight—a love that intensified on the stage." "There was something, absolutely, I loved about the way she moved," Bruhn told Tobi Tobias in an interview about the partnership. "Touching her, just putting a hand, there, without sound, just

Duration of partnership: 1962–63, 1967–71
Companies: La Scala Opera Ballet, American Ballet Theatre
Principal Ballets: *Coppélia, Giselle, La Sylphide, Romeo and Juliet* pas de deux

Giselle. Photo: Martha Swope

Coppélia. Photo: Martha Swope

understanding. When we understood, we never spoke." Bruhn feels that their real flowering, and real awareness of what they had together, came the following year, when they danced their first *Giselle* together at La Scala. "The moment was there and we were both prepared for it."

Despite this momentous rapport, the two dancers' careers took them separate ways until 1967, when Bruhn agreed to return to American Ballet Theatre on the condition that he could have Fracci as his partner. It was here that they consolidated their partnership and took their place together in the minds and hearts of the public. They first appeared in one of their most moving collaborations, *Giselle.*

"[Bruhn] moves like Albrecht, he thinks like Albrecht, and he carries his audience with a gesture. One fear-shot glance conveys a novel, one tense jump becomes a lyric poem. He seems a man shocked by destiny, and his eyes look sadly heroic." Glenna Syse noted the same subtle shading of character in Fracci's performance. "Miss Fracci at first look is all blush and heartbeat . . . still there is always just the hint of the unkind fate ahead, a trace of the foreboding future. It comes with the faintest touch against a pale cheek and a moment of disbelief and nervousness at her good fortune." The partnership was perfect to "the smallest detail," she wrote, and the pair's ability to invest small details with enormous emotional significance was one of the most moving things about them. Another was their rapport. In his book *Erik Bruhn: Danseur Noble,* John Gruen quotes Bruhn on the problem he had doing *Giselle* with an earlier partner, Nora Kaye. "She kept saying she knew the role and that I knew the role too. I would tell her that we *both* would have to know our roles *together* so that they would work well between us." It was precisely this sense of shared vision, a shared world,

La Sylphide. Photo: Martha Swope

that Fracci and Bruhn communicated to each other and to the audience. "We caught fire from each other," Bruhn explains. Fracci says simply, "We were on stage and we were both, together."

There is a relationship between *Giselle* and the other ballet for which Fracci and Bruhn are legendary, *La Sylphide*. Both are products of the Romantic period in ballet and therefore the perfect vehicles for these most Romantic of dancers. Both concern love, betrayal, and death, but, more specifically, are about the relationship of a passionate man with a supernatural woman he can never really possess. Erik Bruhn's Albrecht was particularly driven and obsessed with what Elena Bivona called "a devouring fixation." His James was the same sort of character, but whereas in *Giselle,* his belief in the ideal saves his life, in *La Sylphide,* it kills him. In an article for *Dance Perspectives,* Bruhn discussed his conception of the role. "He is an idealist, a poet. In the end when he tries to grasp his ideal and tries to make her a real woman, he dies . . . Nobody can actually get hold of James . . . But when he is alone with his dream he is quite himself; he is a total being."

Bruhn's James never seemed more complete—and more pathetic—than when he was pursuing Fracci's Sylphide. The role of the Sylph is not a dramatic, three-dimensional (with a little bit of the fourth dimension) role like that of Giselle. Instead, the dancer is called upon to make something memorable out of such delicate and intangible qualities as sweetness and lightness. Fracci, with her painterly looks, enchanting smile, and air of radiance, was perfect, and the pair made another triumph. "Bruhn . . . danced the part of the Scotsman . . . with his own personal intensity coupled with a command of romantic ballet style unequalled by any other dancer," enthused Walter Terry. He continued, "Fracci, who looks as if she had stepped from the frame of a delicately tinted lithograph of the last century, is soft of movement, airy, shy, utterly feminine."

Giselle and *La Sylphide* were the staples of the Fracci-Bruhn repertory during the four years in which they were guest artists with American Ballet Theatre and elsewhere before Erik Bruhn retired from dancing in 1971. (He returned to the stage in 1975, but chiefly in dramatic roles. He and Fracci danced briefly in *The Moor's Pavane* in 1978.)

In 1968, they filmed *Giselle* and in a review by Maria Harriton were praised for their "rare artistry," "focus and style, shape and substance, and heartbreaking emotional power." But the pair had two more strings to their bow. They first danced Bruhn's *Romeo and Juliet* pas de deux on a Bell Telephone Hour program called "The Many Faces of

Flower Festival in Genzano, pas de deux. Photo: Martha Swope

Romeo and Juliet" and later with American Ballet Theatre. With its yearning lifts and sweeping bends, it gave audiences a chance to see the couple in a more modern vein and to see their famous romantic rapport translated into physical rapture.

They also had a success, surprising in a pair of romantic exemplars, in the vigorous comedy *Coppélia.* Fracci, as Swanhilda, was praised as "pert . . . impudent, and defiant," and the very real bond between the two dancers enabled them to convey the confident and tender love between the hero and heroine which exists beneath all the roughhousing.

It wasn't long before Fracci and Bruhn were second only to Fonteyn and Nureyev in their capacity to generate delirious excitement in the theatre. Anna Kisselgoff described a typical reaction. "Their performances cause fans to gasp, cheer, shriek, even travel from Manhattan to Brooklyn, and above all, keep the house packed. When they finished their first *Giselle* . . . carnations, roses, chrysanthemums rained down upon the stage." Marilyn Hunt remembered Brooklyn Academy, where they often performed with American Ballet Theatre, as "a palace where they reigned together, and a home to which one returned to visit them as Giselle and Albrecht or the Sylph and James." At the peak of their mutual career, Hubert Saal wrote this piquant description of their effect:

Romeo and Juliet Pas De Deux. Photo: Fred Fehl

"The partnership between Fracci and Bruhn rivals that of Fonteyn and Nureyev. Bruhn handles Fracci like a soufflé, lifts her like a toast; they exchange look for look, step for step, touch for touch, in perfect rapport, and when he kisses her, her toes curl."

Triumph and notoriety left everyone, including Fracci and Bruhn, trying to analyze what happened. An entry in *Current Biography* hit on part of the truth. "Each released in the other an acute awareness of the performing moment, and because of their responsiveness to each other, one could introduce variations in steps to which the other would be immediately receptive." Spontaneity and freshness were keynotes of Fracci-Bruhn performances. They seemed to be creating themselves—and their roles—anew each time they danced. "I can only say that every time we danced, something new took place," said Fracci. As with the Fonteyn-Nureyev partnership to which it was often compared, this pairing gained from the contrasts of opposite qualities. "It was the contrast that caused the spark between Rudi and Margot," says Bruhn, "and I think that Carla and I had that same spark." It wasn't only the contrast of Nordic cool with Italian warmth, of fair and dark coloring, or technical perfection with expansive dramatic ease, but the special nurturing one of the experienced with the fresh. Bruhn supported and encouraged Fracci, and she in turn renewed and gave new dramatic focus to a man who had always suffered more than most from self-doubt and performance

nerves. At an age when he might otherwise have considered retiring, Bruhn was able to say, "It is Carla who keeps me alive as a dancer. When you dance with someone you respect and like, then each one challenges the other. It sustains a balance and you want to do better. I don't hold back. There is a release. Finally, I'm not as harried to dance alone. I'm dancing for Carla. I'm not saying, 'Oh my God, here comes my variation.'"

But what added depth to the excitement of contrast was a fundamental similarity of approach. Steps were never just steps to Fracci and Bruhn—they were the essence of character. Sydney Johnson wrote of Bruhn's James, "Every step and every gesture seems to be an essential part of the character's performance." And Fracci has said that she must feel the dramatic motivation for everything she does. Fracci and Bruhn were given the Dance Magazine Award in 1973. In presenting the award to Fracci, Antony Tudor commented on "the mysterious sense of being possessed which existed in her performances." This is something both dancers had, an intensity and absorption in their roles and in each other. Bruhn says, "We who work on the stage have a tendency to only contemplate our navels—to be totally self involved. At the same time, we are supposed to be all-giving." Fracci and Bruhn managed triumphantly to be both, and every occasion with them was, as Glenna Syse wrote of *Giselle,* "Always . . . a portrayal, not a performance."

Antoinette Sibley & Anthony Dowell

Felix Mendelssohn's clichéd "Wedding March" was given a new lease on life in 1964 when it was used by Sir Frederick Ashton in *The Dream* to introduce a marriage made in heaven—the partnership of Antoinette Sibley and Anthony Dowell. "Rarely have two dancers been so perfectly matched in physique, temperament and schooling," wrote P. W. Manchester: "the female and male counterpart of exactly the same approach to dance."

Sibley and Dowell first discovered their unique affinity at a rehearsal of Kenneth MacMillan's *Symphony*. Sibley was second cast but had no partner with whom to rehearse the tricky pas de deux, and she asked the dark young man at the back, whom she recognized vaguely as a new member of the company, to "literally hold me up." Romeo and Juliet, whom the pair would later portray so movingly, could scarcely have experienced a greater revelation. "Immediately it all seemed to work," said Sibley, "as though we had been dancing together all of our lives . . . it all seemed effortless." "She was perfect for me," says Dowell. Sibley was the more astonished of the two. Being older and more experienced, she had already danced with all the male leads in the company and knew how rare a perfect harmony of mind and body was.

Though neither dancer mentioned their discovery to anyone, something about them had stirred Frederick Ashton's sixth sense, and he began to choreograph *The Dream* on them. "He has this eye," Sibley says. And where she and Dowell were concerned it was an inner eye. Ashton saw before anyone else what a potent combination they would be, and in *The Dream* he drew out and enshrined their most compelling qualities. "It was very much the

The Sleeping Beauty. Photo: Jennie Walton

"One never had to work at the partnership, it was such a natural thing."

—Antoinette Sibley

essence of both of us," says Dowell. "We both have this slightly arrogant and otherworldly quality," Sibley comments, "and the ability to get this strange supernatural feeling in our dancing." At early rehearsals the dancers assumed they were playing one of the two pairs of lovers, but, though no one actually told them, it soon became obvious that they had the leading roles of Oberon and Titania. As the embattled fairy king and queen whose quarrel is resolved in a pas de deux, Sibley and Dowell combined passion with otherworldly mystery, glamour, and aloofness. They added to this a beauty and symmetry of line that made it possible for the dancing to become, as well as to symbolize, the emotional resolution of the piece. Dale Harris called the pas de deux "one of Ashton's most profound statements on the nature of love." It is full of parallel movements,

---

Duration of partnership: 1965–75
Company: The Royal Ballet
Principal Ballets: *Afternoon of a Faun, Anastasia, Daphnis and Chloe, The Dream, Giselle, Manon, Meditation from Thaïs, The Nutcracker, Pavane, Romeo and Juliet, The Sleeping Beauty, Swan Lake*

The Dream. Photo: Zoë Dominic

simultaneous arabesques and circles completed by the two bodies moving together. The statement, given its highest form by the perfect accord of Sibley and Dowell, was clearly that love is a matter of the mutual surrender of two equals. And so, in this case, was partnership. The two dancers were, in Nicholas Dromgoole's words, "emerging not just as an outstanding ballerina or an outstanding *danseur noble,* but that magical, extra achievement . . . an equal partnership, so perfectly complementing each other their dance seems to have an extra dimension."

Sibley and Dowell had their new-found rapport put to the test the following year when they danced the leads in Kenneth MacMillan's *Romeo and Juliet* and had for the first time to sustain a current of feeling for an entire three-act ballet. They succeeded beautifully, and critics particularly noted how clearly the choreography shone through their detailed and finished performances. This, which Mary Clarke described as "the winged beauty of their dancing," became a special feature of Sibley-Dowell performances. Audiences came away with a heightened awareness of movement and spatial harmony. Sibley and Dowell were the highest manifestations of the English style with its emphasis on delicacy of phrasing, purity of line, and an absolute musical fidelity.

Old classics looked new-minted when Sibley and Dowell danced them. They were dubious about *The Sleeping Beauty* because of its lack of drama and emphasis on technical perfection, but it was a perfect showcase for the way in which their classicism went beyond technique and became instinct. For Peter Wright's new production in 1968, Ashton composed a special "awakening" pas de deux for them, which provided an intimate moment in the grand Petipa framework. "Dowell bears Sibley aloft in big sailing movements," reported Richard Buckle. "Each has a superb solo; then as the stage darkens he sweeps her up and off into the light. This is thrilling." In the grand pas de deux, "Dowell leaps with incredible soaring nobility; Sibley trips ecstatically."

The same ease was noticed by Anna Kisselgoff when the couple danced *Swan Lake* in New York. "Mr. Dowell, leaping higher than ever, turning even more slowly in the difficult multiple pirouettes, and Miss Sibley, simply splendid in technique, are so clearly at ease in the grandeur of the classic pas de deux that they turn them into highly expressive drama with seemingly no effort."

Giselle was a special experience for them, the classic that seemed to unite them fully. Sibley had always adored it. As someone who had had frail health for years, and who was an all-or-nothing romantic, she sympathized with the betrayed peasant. "For anyone who

believes so totally, the deception when discovered can break their heart . . . it is not a fairy story . . . it is something real about grief, and loss and love," Sibley has said. Dowell, with his combination of reticence and passion, and the noble and brooding good looks associated with romantic princes, was perfect as an Albrecht keeping his double life at bay. "A very great performance," wrote G. B. L. Wilson, "and it sets the seal on their partnership; for the next five years or more British ballet lies in their hands." Offstage Sibley and Dowell were and are "the greatest friends." They always added an offstage dimension of fun and togetherness to any project they embarked upon. In the case of *Giselle,* Dowell arranged Sibley's hair, as he was later to design a number of their costumes.

If the classics were the foundation stones of the Royal Ballet style, its architect was Frederick Ashton, and Sibley and Dowell were at their very best in Ashton works. When they did *Cinderella,* Clive Barnes wrote, "Mr. Dowell and Miss Sibley go together like a pair of singing birds." And they captured to perfection the delicate emotions of the pastoral romance *Daphnis and Chloe.* Sibley's generously pretty face and a certain irrepressible quality and Dowell's fleet and vivid dancing made the characters memorable. "They were born to be pastoral lovers," observed Barnes, "and Ashton's choreography is first nature to them. . . . Sibley is innocent and sensual . . . Mr. Dowell is a beautifully ardent dancer—his nerve ends are in his technique."

Those nerve ends were exposed and the pair's cool beauty of line pared down to its essence in two of Jerome Robbins's ballets. Of *Dances at a Gathering,* Richard Buckle wrote, "In the Etude . . . Sibley and Dowell, divinely matched, kneel, stand still as the music sweeps by, then join it in a big dance . . . [They] are always magical together." And of their balletic brief encounter in *Afternoon of a Faun,* "At last Debussy gives the cue—it is summer, after all—the boy kisses the girl's cheek. You might think such a thing had never happened to either of them before. . . . Sibley and Dowell were beautiful together." "The emotions are balanced on a knife edge," observed Nicholas Dromgoole.

There was an uncanny psychic dimension to the Sibley and Dowell partnership, which had something to do with their proportions and the way they hear music ("but *absolutely* the same," says Sibley) and something to do with an unanalyzable intuitive sympathy. "He knew, or could tell, how I was going to reach at the end of a movement, or pick me up in the middle of something because he knew that that was where I was going. It was so natural, we

Meditation from Thaïs. Photo: Leslie Spatt

wouldn't have to talk about things, we'd just know about things." And Dowell says he is fascinated when he looks at performance pictures and notices that in poses held "sometimes literally for split seconds," the two of them are identical.

This intuitive sympathy works offstage as well as on, and Sibley tells a funny story about a recent lunch date when she and Dowell arrived at the appointed restaurant carrying identical white plastic bags containing copies of their book *(Sibley and Dowell,* with Nicholas Dromgoole) a fan wanted autographed. Not only did they both have the same bags ("I never have white plastic bags," says Sibley), but both had dithered about bringing the book to a restaurant, and both produced the same apology. "It was just one of those extraordinary things again," says Sibley. "We looked at each other and burst out laughing. You can't explain things like that. We'd do that sort of thing all the time when we were dancing."

Choreographers liked to use Sibley and Dowell's parallelism. In his staging of *The Nutcracker,* Rudolf Nureyev created a pas de deux on the pair that began with sweeping simultaneous arm movements. Alexander Bland wrote, "When they . . . danced in parallel, as

Nureyev likes to make them, they were like the two wings of an invisible soaring bird." This pas de deux had its luster dimmed at one performance when the evil mice of the story pulled Sibley's whole skirt away and she had to carry on in tights, with Dowell, the model prince, looking aghast. He values a sense of humor in partnerships, and they always giggle about mishaps like this. *The Dream*, Ashton's "awakening" pas de deux in *Sleeping Beauty*, and his *Thaïs* and Kenneth MacMillan's *Manon* were other works that contained mirror image

effects for Sibley and Dowell. These became, in a way, one of the partnership's trademarks, as an entry in *Current Biography* noted. "The duo's smooth and lucid dancing can perhaps be best appreciated when they execute the same steps in parallel movement." Where many partnerships are a matter of discussion, or opposition, or emotional continuity, Sibley and Dowell were almost unique in their physical harmony. Dowell said, "When working on new roles, the successful version of the step or lift is always arrived at by letting our bodies

Afternoon of a Faun. Photo: Leslie Spatt

sort it out—without our minds." Tobi Tobias defined it as "bodies so attuned to each other that their energy seems to emanate from a single source."

This private bond very soon became public property, and Sibley-and-Dowell were second only to Fonteyn-and-Nureyev in popularity. America particularly wanted to explore the very different style and effect of these two from that of the Royal Ballet's premier couple. A *Dance Magazine* article even called them the "Crown Princess and Prince of English Ballet," and another piece was headed "The Pair Perfect." In a vivid image, Arlene Croce saw Sibley "as the fearless plunging instrument of Dowell's archery." John Gruen wrote a detailed piece for *The New York Times* on "The New Golden Pair": "Sibley and Dowell find that mysterious meeting ground that makes of two dancers a single magnetic force. Antoinette Sibley . . . is the essence of the Romantic ballerina. She is at once tender, intense and quixotic, while Anthony Dowell, slim and aristocratic, is the image of the poetic, Byronic, youthful partner. In any pas de deux, there is about them an ardent impetuosity, tempered by a regal sense of inward calm." Whatever it was, audiences loved it. After their last-night *Romeo and Juliet* in New York in 1974, the pair was honored by a twenty-five-minute ovation and banners reading "Sibley and Dowell Forever."

Sibley's romantic, quixotic side as well as what she calls "a certain sensuality" and Dowell's ardent quality were highlighted in Ashton's showpiece pas de deux *Thaïs,* but also particularly in the works Kenneth MacMillan choreographed on them.

Thaïs was worked up very quickly by Ashton for a gala at the Adelphi Theatre. It was a distillation of Oriental glamour, with the sensuousness and glimmer of a Persian miniature. Dowell designed the costumes, and the audience response was so rapturous they had to encore.

In MacMillan's *Anastasia,* the same year, a flash back to the grand old days at the Russian court revealed Sibley as the legendary imperial ballerina Mathilde Kchessinska with Dowell as an anonymous partner. They suggested the opulent grandeur of the originals in their classical pas de deux. MacMillan's pas de deux *Pavane* was in the more lyrical mode, which he used again the following year in the lovers' dances in *Manon* to point up the turbulent melodrama of the plot. Nobody suggests sexuality better than MacMillan, and in Sibley and Dowell he found the perfect embodiment of the passionate and tender but fatally greedy Manon and her sensitive lover Des Grieux. The pas de deux encapsulated their special magic, headlong plunges evolving into delicately beautiful shapes. Sibley says

Manon. Photo: MIRA

she is a "drifter" to whom "things always happen dramatically," and that was the essence of her Manon. Dowell, the technical perfectionist, made his long yearning arabesques as clear as the spoken word. Richard Buckle wrote, "Sibley is admirable as the wanton with a heart of silver-gilt, conveys exactly the battle raging inside her between love and money, looks marvelous both in rags and diamonds and throws herself passionately into the difficult dances." "Dowell . . . is extraordinarily touching and credible" and, recalled Nicholas Dromgoole, "we almost forgot the technical marvels, the elegant fluency of line and control, because each movement took us closer to every innermost thought Des Grieux had."

"I can only say it's what a personality brings out in you," muses Sibley, "what you can fight against, what pushes you to your limits and brings out the best in you." "I think [successful partners] feed each other on the stage," says Dowell. For over ten years Sibley and Dowell fed and brought out the best in each other. But the fans wouldn't get their wish—Sibley and Dowell forever. In 1979, Sibley, grounded for three years by a knee injury, announced her retirement. The couple has been reunited occasionally for galas (and for several performances of Robert Helpmann's *Hamlet).* At one of these in 1980, they danced the "Nocturne" pas de deux from *The Dream,* and the audience saw again what people had first seen in 1965: an enchanted grove, an enchanted couple, and, in a moment, something unforgettable about love—and about dancing.

Marcia Haydée & Richard Cragun

In 1969, John Cranko's little-known Stuttgart Ballet took New York by storm and, virtually overnight, the dance partnership of Marcia Haydée and Richard Cragun was thrown into international prominence. It is typical of their unusual impact that the couple first captured the attention of audiences not in a predictably romantic vehicle like *Romeo and Juliet,* but in the athletic and brazenly comic *The Taming of the Shrew.* The couple would prove, over the years, to be enormously successful in a wide range of works, but Cranko's Elizabethan tour de force held a special place in their partnership. The hero and heroine, like the dancers who portrayed them, combined an all-out physicality with a sharp intelligence. At once robust and tender, Haydée and Cragun's Katerina and Petruchio literally disarmed each other into love. It was in *Shrew* that audiences first saw Cragun's astonishing triple air turn (at that time unique among male dancers) and Haydée's staccato legs and vibrant dramatic presence. (In this combination of assets she was a little like Alicia Alonso.)

From the first, Haydée and Cragun's combination of vigor and drama reminded viewers of another great pair. "They must be classed with the finest to be seen in the world of dance," exulted Walter Terry. "These two artists, together, make a brand of theatre magic different from but as potent as, say, that of Fonteyn and Nureyev." Clive Barnes agreed: "In Marcia Haydée and Richard Cragun . . . the company has two international stars fit to shine in the brightest of constellations."

Like Fonteyn and Nureyev, Haydée and Cragun came from two different worlds. Brazilian-born Haydée went from the Royal Ballet School to the corps of Le Grand Ballet du Marquis de Cuevas. When the Marquis died

Duration of partnership: 1962–80
Companies: Stuttgart Ballet, 1962–80; guest appearances with various companies including American Ballet Theatre and the Royal Ballet
Principal Ballets: *Eugene Onegin, Requiem, Romeo and Juliet, Song of the Earth, The Taming of the Shrew, Voluntaries*

Romeo and Juliet. Photo: MIRA

"It's as if we were one person."
—Marcia Haydée

"Good partners give, they do not take. When you're able to let go of your ego, then something magical can happen."
—Richard Cragun

The Taming of the Shrew. Photo: Beverley Gallegos

71

Eugene Onegin, rehearsal. Photo: © 1977 Jack Vartoogian

in 1961, she asked John Cranko if she could audition for the Stuttgart, which he had recently taken over, and was astonished to be chosen as a principal. Haydée, a true Latin, says she believes every artist should have a strong temper and a strong temperament. She has plenty of both.

A year after her engagement by Cranko, the very different Cragun entered the company after a year at the Royal Ballet School. If Haydée was a typical South American, Cragun, with his dark good looks and ingenuous air, seemed at first the archetypal Californian. "I did come across," he observed in an interview, "as this flamingo-chartreuse-straw hat-hip-swinging-tap dancing American." Cragun altered that image considerably over the years, but retained a kind of buoyancy. His earliest fascination had been with Gene Kelly, and he shared with his idol candid charm and a combination of grace and athleticism. In their book *Danseur,* Richard Philp and Mary Whitney describe Cragun as "a sort of Errol Flynn of the dance," and Haydée actually compared him to a luxury car. "His motor is running, like in a fine Mercedes Benz car. You can see there is so much more that is going to come out."

When John Cranko took over the Stuttgart Ballet, he began to create it anew, and very soon Haydée and Cragun—and their partnership—became his chief instruments. Cranko's greatest works combined a challengingly acrobatic style with a formal narrative structure. *The Taming of the Shrew, Romeo and Juliet,* and *Eugene Onegin* required a complete fusion of dance and drama, and in this his premier pair excelled. "Everything must happen together," Haydée has asserted. "Each step must somehow reflect something in the characters. Otherwise, things like a pas de deux have no meaning." Haydée and Cragun's pas de deux overflowed with meaning. Not long after Cragun joined the company, the couple began a long-term personal relationship which added depth to their interactions on stage. Everything they did was charged with tenderness and excitement. Ballerina Cynthia Gregory has commented, "Such rapport is very rare. I saw it . . . in Stuttgart between Marcia Haydée and Richard Cragun, and I saw how beautifully John Cranko used it in his work."

Doris Hering, too, noticed the highly personal nature of their stage lives in an article about Haydée. "With Richard Cragun there are games to be played, flirtations to be consummated, his crackling athleticism to be answered. When I see Haydée with Cragun [I] remember Fonteyn with Nureyev."

The Taming of the Shrew was a unique triumph for the pair, but they excelled, too, in both more and much less conventionally romantic material. They were widely praised in Cranko's *Romeo and Juliet.* Haydée, gauntly beautiful, seemed to burn with a flame in which the hesitations of girlhood were burned away in the passions of womanhood. Cragun answered her with boyish ardor and vital physicality. "Miss Haydée is a Juliet so young, so vulnerable, so captured by love that you will never forget her. And Cragun is the ardent, wild, angry, fierce, and enraptured Romeo," Walter Terry averred. Clive Barnes agreed, "Marcia Haydée is an adorable Juliet—she looks like a painting and dances like a lyric poem. Her emotions are naked and her

Voluntaries. Photo: Beverley Gallegos

dancing explores them with a transparent fury. . . . [Cragun's] dancing is remarkable, and his ardor as convincing as totally felt young love itself. . . . Cranko could not have found two more happy yet more tragic lovers. Every gesture realizes his ideal."

Haydée and Cragun were able to turn from the innocent love portrayed in *Romeo and Juliet* to the twisted and thwarted passions of *Eugene Onegin.* Though Cragun was not in the original cast he gave a powerful performance as the cynical and alienated Onegin, and Haydée as the infatuated Tatiana made Walter Terry describe her as a "dance tragedienne in the great tradition of Nora Kaye."

Haydée and Cragun in fact appeared in the work most associated with Kaye when they danced *Pillar of Fire* with American Ballet Theatre. Of Haydée, Frances Herridge wrote, "Her expressive body flowed through the phrases like quicksilver," and Cragun was powerful as her indifferent seducer. The pair, who were so at one with each other, were equally good at suggesting joyous love and morbid obsession. Two other works Cranko made on them were the sunny *Daphnis and Chloe* and the eerie work *Traces,* about a concentration camp survivor haunted by the memory of her dead husband.

In an interview in John Gruen's *The Private World of Ballet,* Haydée once described her mentor Cranko as a man who "can dream up steps that are absolutely dazzling. I mean, he will ask you to do things that you *know* are impossible to execute. But miraculously, you *can* do them." Cragun analyzed the essence of Cranko's work by noting that his characters are "going through a cycle of life, trying to make some kind of contact." Haydée and Cragun managed to be, on one hand, accomplished technicians doing the impossible for Cranko, and on the other, always suggesting the warm human current in any work, "combining," as Tobi Tobias wrote "acrobatic daring with vivid emotional force." One reason was their mutual admiration and trust.

"I think that a partnership results when two people are mature enough to give of themselves," said Cragun. "Good partners *give,* they do not take. When you're able to let go of your ego, then something magical can happen."

"It's as if we were one person," continued Haydée. "Ricky knows me so well. He knows where I am, where my balance is, what I need, what I don't need. I never worry with Ricky. I just throw myself on him, and I know that if something goes wrong, he'll do something to make it right." (She was being modest. As Doris Hering observed "Haydée must . . . be heaven to partner, for she moves with the concealed relaxation of a cat.")

As a result of this sympathetic bond, their performances, as John Gruen observed, "assured clarity and refinement of execution that moves beyond mere technique . . . one is in contact with the process of the creative act."

Under Cranko, the Haydée-Cragun collaboration gained international recognition. One sign of their "arrival" in the public eye was a *Vogue* photo essay with pictures by Richard Avedon and the caption "She is all mind and legs. He is lavishly physical. Together they have fire and delicacy, an enticement for the eyes."

They enticed in England as well as America (Richard Buckle announced that he would "swim the Rhine to see Haydée and Cragun knocking each other about [in *Shrew*] any day") and were much in demand for galas.

John Cranko's new classics were the staple of the Stuttgart repertory, but Haydée and Cragun also danced in plotless works like Cranko's own *Initials R.B.M.E.* (a dance homage to his chief dancers Cragun, Birgit Keil, Haydée, and Egon Madsen) and Kenneth MacMillan's stark and compelling *Song of the Earth.* After Cranko's unexpected death in 1973, Glen Tetley was for a short time Stuttgart's director. More abstract works entered the repertory, and Haydée and Cragun were particularly striking in his semireligious ballet memorial to Cranko, *Voluntaries.* Several years later, MacMillan mourned Cranko in his *Requiem,* and Haydée and Cragun became symbols of grief and acceptance.

In plotless works, Haydée and Cragun's physical disparity highlighted their unity on the stage. Haydée, tiny, sharp, fierce, and birdlike, became tender and yielding with Cragun. He, massive and muscled, was like a pliant statue, each movement clearly articulated, yet flowing. In *Song of the Earth,* in which they represented all men and all women in the face of Death, Haydée had, according to Fernau Hall, "a strangely powerful, yet tender radiance about her," and Cragun was "superb as her alter ego, his splendidly masculine presence a perfect foil for her lambent femininity." Doris Hering recorded the striking image they projected in *Voluntaries,* one which seems to sum up the partnership as well as the dance: "Finally there was a duet . . . in which their tumult was resolved into soft turns through which he bore her lightly and then shifted her body until she became his wings."

The raw physical self, visible beneath the surface decorum of the narrative-dramatic ballets, was completely exposed in works like these, and once again Haydée and Cragun compressed the physical and emotional elements into a single force. As John Gruen observed, ". . . an intoxicating dislocation makes itself felt . . . the image of movement coalesces into pure emotion." And because this is the most satisfactory effect a theatrical experience can produce, Marcia Haydée and Richard Cragun were, as Gruen continued, a partnership "rooted in the inevitable, like something that was simply meant to be."

Daphnis and Chloe. Photo: Beverley Gallegos

Patricia McBride & Edward Villella

"... power matched to power, will to will, in an unresolvable contest."
—Elena Bivona
"We had so much fun together."
—Patricia McBride

"Complete and total pleasure," was how Edward Villella described dancing. And complete and total pleasure was what he and Patricia McBride offered audiences when they danced together. They were ballet's first all-Americans, dazzling and vivacious, and their partnership was a true democracy, a genial battle of wit and will on equal terms. "The exuberance of their energy matched," wrote Tobi Tobias in *Dance Magazine*. "Villella's intense, theatrical athleticism teamed with McBride's bold good looks, her vivacious physical self-sufficiency, seemed to typify a new breed of American classical dancer."

These two exemplars of the new American classicism had typically American childhoods. McBride was born in Teaneck, New Jersey, and Villella in Bayside, New York, where he played baseball as well as taking ballet classes. Both attended the School of American Ballet, and McBride feels that part of their rapport was grounded in this common training. "Eddie and I grew up in the company together," she told Tobi Tobias.

Villella was already a principal dancer and rapidly becoming a star, even in the starless New York City Ballet, when McBride joined the company at sixteen. Although Villella had lost four vital years of training while he attended college, when he finally returned to dancing he regained lost ground with astonishing facility. His blazing determination not only made him succeed, it became part of his dancing persona, and it was soon answered by an equal fire from McBride.

One of the first works the pair appeared in

Duration of partnership: 1963–76
Companies: New York City Ballet, 1963–76; guest appearances with André Eglevsky Company and others and concert tours with own group
Principal Ballets: *Afternoon of a Faun, Dances at a Gathering, Harlequinade, Jewels* ("Rubies"), *A Midsummer Night's Dream, The Nutcracker, Tarantella,* Tchaikovsky *Pas De Deux*

together was John Taras's *Fantasy,* a ballet in the Romantic manner, in which a young girl, transformed into a witchlike creature by the moon, watches while her lover is killed by ten "Watchers of the Night" (reminiscent of *Giselle's* wilis). McBride and Villella were praised by Walter Terry for combining atmosphere and technique. "Patricia McBride . . . as the gloriously lovely creature who turns into a witch, not only excites the viewer with her powers in projecting the macabre, but also dazzles the eye with a series of tours en attitude which are nothing less than fabulous. [Villella] as the damned youth . . . acts with conviction and performs with technical élan."

McBride and Villella undertook to create another atmosphere, of remembrance of things past, in a revival of Antony Tudor's *Dim Lustre* in which they played a pair of socialites recalling episodes in their pasts.

But these two ballets were not characteristic of the McBride-Villella partnership. They excelled in things that were direct and vivid, not oblique, and George Balanchine created a number of works to take advantage of their energy and wit.

Bravado was natural to Villella—he was a street-wise danseur—and he began to draw out McBride, who began her career as a cautious classicist, hiding her light under a bushel. Both dancers were small and, in motion, hyperkinetic, with so much energy and flexibility they seemed to suspend natural physical laws. Both had dark, alert features and ready smiles, as if a master painter had set brush right to canvas. They had a friskiness and urchin charm perfectly captured in Balanchine's first work for them, the peasant pas de deux *Tarantella.* This demi-caractère gem was a whirlwind of non-stop movement. Arms, legs, head, neck, hands, and tambourines all flew. McBride and Villella literally kicked up their heels and danced with looks of glee, as if astonished by their own capacities. Edward Barry wrote, "Controlled hysteria is the essence of the tarantella . . . Patricia McBride and Edward Villella . . . surrendered themselves to the intoxication of the rhythm." Surrender was one aspect of their style, and so was competitiveness, as one critic, who praised *Tarantella's* "witty match-and-meet-steps," noted.

If *Tarantella* was a compressed character sketch, *Harlequinade* was a full-scale

Harlequinade. Photo: Martha Swope

Tarantella. Photo: Martha Swope

realization of the *commedia dell'arte* style, with Balanchinian accents, and Villella and McBride were this ballet cake's spice and icing as the incorrigibly mischievous Harlequin and Columbine.

There has probably not been so natural a Harlequin since Nijinsky. The bounding leaps, the shrugs, the sly twinkles came to Villella like breathing, and McBride's dainty Columbine combined sweetness with wit. Balanchine and his dancers combined sugar and steel—Pollock's Toy Theatre met the Maryinsky—and McBride and Villella once again allied demi-caractère charm with breathtaking modern virtuosity.

"Edward Villella was the bounding hero," reported Walter Terry, "and not only did he cut loose with some fabulous feats of skill, but he also played the role of Harlequin with a fine awareness of both the ardor and the humor inherent in the part. He was matched by the lovely Patricia McBride, who also acted as skillfully as she danced, and that, I might add, is something to shout about."

Don McDonagh was equally enthusiastic. "Mr. Villella danced a Harlequin like Horatio Alger on a hot tin roof, and Miss McBride as

Columbine allied her glittering presence to his brash ardor to produce a dance union of inescapable charm."

"Wit" was a word used frequently to describe the character of McBride-Villella performances, and nowhere did it shine more brilliantly than in the shrill, jazzy, outrageous, and technically extraordinary "Rubies" section of *Jewels.* Like the Stravinsky music it used, "Rubies" combined elements of the clownish and the profound. McBride and Villella, in roles that called for outrageous feats of speed and strength, dazzling turns and spins, combined with satirical humor, were unmatched—except by each other. "Rubies" was a fight to the finish in which both were triumphant, "a partnership between equals," as Arlene Croce wrote, who "matched wits in a power play." "Rubies" is without characters, but suggests a wide range of characters. The leads are show girls, gymnasts, bicyclists, gang leaders, playing with classical style confidently, and all the while suggesting amused camaraderie. "Together they create a spirited game of boy meets girl that combines the blatantly athletic with the buoyantly aesthetic." But McBride and Villella could never be just any boy and girl. "Mary Astor besting Bogart," concluded Croce.

Villella said of McBride, "She always had this wit in her dancing. She was secure enough in her steps to project a sense of humor." This was true of him as well, and it is one reason why the pair did so well in the comic ballets.

They fought another battle royal in *A Midsummer Night's Dream* when McBride came to dance the role of Titania opposite Villella's Oberon. (In Sir Frederick Ashton's version, this ballet enshrined another partnership, that of Sibley and Dowell.) Concentrated, their vitality becomes implacable authority, their wit, a wicked humor. Like "Rubies," it was another case of "power matched to power, will to will, in an unresolvable contest," as Elena Bivona wrote. "Their initial meeting, with its frozen hostility, always suggests a battle and mutually played tricks that have been enlivening the forest for aeons."

McBride and Villella's special qualities suggested the ballets created for them by Balanchine, but they also enhanced the other works they danced in the New York City Ballet repertory. Neither dancer was built ideally for classical roles. They were small, and McBride had a deeply curved back and prominent head, while Villella was very muscular and compact and had to combat stiffness resulting from strain and injury. They were unorthodox dancers, and in classical roles they made unorthodoxy their strength. In place of perfect line, they had radiance and compelling glamour. McBride could accent movement

Dim Lustre. Photo: Martha Swope

beautifully, and Villella always made steps larger and fiercer than they had ever been. Above all, they were entirely at one—the perfect equals who created their own kingdom. "It's necessary to be with the partner you're dancing with 100%," says McBride.

"Put McBride and Villella in *Nutcracker,* beyond battles," wrote Elena Bivona in *Ballet Review,* "and they are the radiant vision of a union rejoicing in its perfect wholeness, and the grandeur of it fulfills the ballet's dream of true civilization." As a last-minute replacement cast for the more established team of Hayden

"Rubies," from *Jewels.* Photo: Martha Swope

and d'Amboise in *Swan Lake,* McBride and Villella drew raves from Walter Terry. McBride, he wrote, "is beautiful in body and in face and she moves with incredible poetry of motion as she defines, swiftly or with superb legato, breathtaking designs in space . . . Edward Villella danced with brilliance, as he always does . . . a truly memorable *Swan Lake.*"

One of their greatest triumphs came in Balanchine's Tchaikovsky *Pas de Deux.* A frank showpiece, large-scale and gleaming with classical tradition, it can be everything or nothing, depending on the performers. McBride and Villella danced it on the New York City Ballet's twentieth anniversary and, as Elena Bivona reports, it was everything. "The victory of equilibrium over difficulties . . . When the ballet was over I was laughing, surrounded by laughing, shouting people who looked at each other for joy, to see reflections of it next to them."

One of the couple's greatest gifts to their public was this communicable exhilaration, and they soon began to take it outside the company, becoming, like many famous couples before them, ambassadors for their art. Villella organized concert tours, and they performed at Jacob's Pillow, Lewisohn Stadium, with the Eglevsky Ballet, and as far away as Lebanon. Once they danced at Saratoga with the entire Philadelphia Orchestra—a first. Their repertory included *Le Corsaire* and the "Bluebird" pas de deux (which they also danced on the Bell Telephone Hour), as well as staples from the New York City Ballet repertory and original pieces by Villella. They put their individual stamp on everything they did ("Part of the pleasure of their performances is this explicit glorifying in their own identities," observed Ann Barzel), and in some cases, it had no equal. Reviewing a White Plains appearance in which they danced the *Tchaikovsky Pas De Deux* and *Raymonda Variations,* Clive Barnes wrote unequivocally, "For a few moments while they were dancing last night, one knew with certainty that at that instant there could be no better dancing taking place anywhere else in the world."

One of McBride and Villella's ventures was tours of city schools, where they gave lecture-demonstrations to crowds of skeptical, if not downright hostile teenagers, to whom ballet was ludicrous and effeminate. In a documentary about Villella, *Man Who Dances,* we can see how one group of kids changes its attitudes from mirth to respect to awe as Villella talks, and he and McBride demonstrate and finally perform, a dazzling *Tchaikovsky Pas De Deux.*

There was a lyrical side to McBride and Villella that came out particularly in Jerome

Dances at a Gathering. Photo: Martha Swope

Robbins's ballets *Afternoon of a Faun* and *Dances at a Gathering.* There was something elemental about them, which was channeled into verve by a piece like *Tarantella,* but became easy naturalism in Robbins's works. According to the choreographer, Villella was one of the inspirations for *Faun.* His unconscious stretching in class had something "animalistic" about it that appealed to Robbins, and Villella retained it when he came to dance the role. McBride combined an ease of movement with a remote quality that made her nymph as much creature as dancer.

McBride and Villella were the unemphatic center of *Dances at a Gathering,* which had started as a Chopin pas de deux for the two of them. Out of that came the now famous flowering of dance and dancers, but for some, their pas de deux with its elaborate lifts done, as Croce put it, "as casually as one might fold a napkin while speaking," was an enduring image of freedom in difficulty. In a review of the piece, Clive Barnes describes its adherence to Chopin's contradictions, "all daggers and velvet, all poet and peasant," and this coexistence of the lyrical and earthy was what McBride and Villella conveyed so beautifully.

In an interview with Brett Shapiro in *Dance Scope,* Villella defined what makes a dancer special. "The quality of movement is what is distinctive, what gives meaning." The quality of movement that gave meaning to the McBride-Villella partnership combined explosive energy, harnessed by terrific discipline, with an air of ebullience and freedom. "Dance with everything," Balanchine said about *Tarantella,* and they always did, seeming to almost break the confines of movement and spring away altogether. "We had so much fun together," says McBride, and it was clear to all who watched them. The image we have of them is like a kaleidoscope, a wheel of color and motion, always changing, always bringing wit and joy. Like their memorable Tchaikovsky *Pas De Deux* performance their partnership was, in Elena Bivona's words, "the blazing proof she and Villella lit that life can be glorious, and fully sentient."

Apollo. Photo: Martha Swope

exciting . . . it added a whole new aspect to my dancing." "Together Farrell and Martins mesh like an upside/down Fonteyn and Nureyev. Martins's precision holds Farrell in check at the same time that her electricity sparks him off," observed one critic.

George Balanchine brought out this warmer side in his first work for the two of them, the gypsy rhapsody *Tzigane.* Farrell's lush serpentine movements manage to be beautiful while at the same time joking about the slushy romantic nature of gypsy music and dancing. Martins, as her foot-stamping cavalier, seems to join in the fun, head thrown back in the approved swaggering style, every gesture a throb. They work so well together that proximity becomes complicity, and they manage to imply more than is actually in the convention. David Vaughan got the ambiguous feel of *Tzigane* when he recalled "the moment when Farrell ran on pointe in a full backbend over Martins' arm—it was satirical, perhaps, but a breathtaking dance movement too."

In roles like this and the "Fall" pas de deux in Jerome Robbins's *The Four Seasons,* Farrell is more the natural sensualist, Martins the conscious humorist who plays up to her abandon. In Robbins's flagrant Bacchic rite, blazing in flame-colored costumes, the gods were disporting themselves. Arlene Croce observed that Farrell had made this pastiche of opera-ballet allegory into a genuine portrait: "Farrell's great voluptuary is a projection of her virtuoso technical capacities. Her precision . . . is epicurean." She cited Martins as "a superbly sensitive partner." Robert Greskovic called them "distinctly entertaining. Farrell especially for her heart-of-the-matter flamboyance, reckless power and ravishing posture, Martins especially for his superb partnering."

But Martins is far more than a mere support for Farrell. His technique is so perfect and his stage presence so larger-than-life that he commands attention every minute, and Farrell is large enough a dancer not to be diminished by a partner for whom background and foreground are the same. "Together," wrote Richard Poirier, "Martins and Farrell are, at their best, the most brilliant partners in the world of dance. Her strength, abandon and virtuosity are like a direct challenge to the measured grandeur of his deportment; she brings out the fullness of his power. They challenge one another, but they do not actually compete."

If Farrell and Martins are an "upside/down Fonteyn and Nureyev," they are also, in many ways, the reverse of another great City Ballet pair, McBride and Villella. While the latter, compact and fleet, were earthy, open, and direct, giving performances that washed over you like a wave, Farrell and Martins seem to unfold slowly before us. Each movement is spacious and deliberate, yet they build up tremendous excitement by giving us a number of oblique angles that slowly add up to a whole picture that lingers in the mind.

"Here is a filtered view of Odette," wrote Anne Kisselgoff in a review of *Swan Lake,* "with her head in the crook of her arm, her arched arabesques with arms back and swoons taken at an amazing new tilt . . . Miss Farrell, dancing with both daring and graciousness, and Mr. Martins have appeared in these roles many times . . . their performance could only be equated with greatness." In Robbins's *In G Major,* the whole ballet seems to unfold slowly from their central pas de deux with its furling and unfurling movements, as if they were creating it anew. It is a particular celebration of their physical harmony. "Her body resembles my body," says Martins. "She moves in the same long, swinging way I do. Enormous span. Long legs." (There is an e. e. cummings poem that begins, "i like my body when it is with your / body. It is so quite new a thing. / Muscles better and nerves more.") As a pair, they are the highest realization of Balanchine's ideal of classicism in the way they are able to give old forms new accent. This shows clearly in works like the "Diamonds" section of *Jewels.* It is a miniature "white act" of a traditional classical ballet, harking back to the style of the Maryinsky in which Balanchine was nurtured. In its purity, it threatens blandness, but with Farrell and Martins it is a breathtaking experience. Each movement is lingered over and amplified, and each dancer seems to contribute to the other even when standing still. The space between them is electric, and they are regal. "What they have as partners is what makes them both brilliant soloists: total attention to dynamics," wrote Elizabeth Kendall. "Both have superb bravura technique at their command, but both choose to subordinate a moment, no matter how sensational, to the overall design of the dance." Balanchine, with his predominantly neoclassical plotless repertory and his emphasis on what Martins calls "pure dancing, no fuss, no banalities," has in these two dancers the perfect combination—instruments who are also creators.

Of course, when pure sensation is called for, as in the bravura Tchaikovsky *Pas De Deux,* Farrell and Martins can certainly deliver. "They brought the house down," reported Anna Kisselgoff after one performance. "The way her loose-flung abandon matched Mr. Martins's precision is what made the pas de deux so exciting on this occasion. It was a matter of contrasts." With this piece they were also the hit of the 1976 Royal Ballet gala at the Royal Opera House.

Along with their regality, serenity, and

Afternoon of a Faun. Photo: Martha Swope

assurance, Farrell and Martins project an air of privacy. McBride and Villella opened their arms and invited us into their world. With these two, it is something we have come upon by chance—a room, a grove, a corner of Olympus. Charged with this privacy, the torturous, twisty pas de deux in *Agon,* performed with remote aplomb, seems at once a public contest and a private ritual ("He seems to 'exercise' her body," comments Richard Poirier, "to test its potentialities") as does, in another way, the brief encounter between rehearsing dancers in Robbins's *Afternoon of a Faun.* Farrell and Martins's performances never show you everything at once. They hint and have a resonance that remains long after they are gone. Poirier calls it "art as an inquiry into the mystery of things." They are the perfect couple for the divertissement pas de deux in Balanchine's *A Midsummer Night's Dream.* In its complete abstraction from the plot, it is the one symbol of perfect love in the ballet. It begins with the dancers alone in the corner of stage with their backs to the audience, and so eloquent are Farrell and Martins in this moment that we know, however dazzling and "public" the rest of the piece is, that it is something unique and private to them. "Farrell and Martins have reached a rare balance between visible stage daring and profound stage manners," writes Elizabeth Kendall.

The way the two dancers excite and fulfill each other has an effect on any ballet they appear in, even when they are not directly partners. Martins thinks Balanchine may not have paired them in his *Davidsbündlertänze* because they would be so immediately dominant, and Deborah Trustman describes the moment when they do come together briefly at the end of the work. "For a moment, Peter Martins dances with Suzanne Farrell and the scale—both physical and emotional—changes. Where Martins was distant, he is, for a moment, present and focused; he contains and balances Miss Farrell's expansive elegant movement. It is more than a physical match. The two of them are breathtaking . . . they dominate the stage until they separate, and the spell is broken." Farrell says she trusts Martins "completely as a partner." In her trust is part of the secret of her daring and expansion.

Farrell and Martins create their own environment whenever they dance, but in *Chaconne,* Balanchine set out to give them a special kingdom. Though part of the ballet was originally choreographed in 1963 for the Hamburg Ballet, it looked completely new with the pair and seems to be the quintessential symbol of their partnership. In an article called "A Matched Pair," Elizabeth Kendall analyzed the ballet—and its stars—at length. "*Chaconne* contains the first full roles for the two of them

Tchaikovsky *Pas De Deux.* Photo: Martha Swope

together, and even though the material is not all new, the work seems entirely fresh . . . the ballet looks like it's about these two people." During the first extended pas de deux, "the sight of a tall, splendid Peter Martins supporting a delicate, long-necked Farrell seems mythological. The episode could be a distillation of the Orpheus and Eurydice myth. Or just a dream prelude. It is also a profoundly subtle piece of partnership." In a way, here and in the second, courtly duet, Balanchine makes Farrell's and Martins's subtle partnership as much the subject of the work as anything Gluck's music evokes. In the second pas de deux they are the royal couple so at ease with their regality that they can play with it. Farrell does a flat-footed walk on Martins's arm that suggests a dignified promenade, but has something of a strut about it. In the daring balances, the skimming lifts, they are so at one it's impossible to distinguish the source of movement. "Who's to know whether it's her leg . . . or Martins's arms that are doing the most propelling," observed Nancy Goldner. "Farrell's steps are full of surprising new twists; her aplomb is sublime," wrote Croce. "And Martins achieves a rhythmic plangency that is independently thrilling. (When people speak of him as the perfect partner for Farrell, this is not all they mean, but it's part of it.)" Goldner's unequivocal announcement that Farrell and Martins were "the world's two most gorgeous dancers" suggests the opulent perfection they projected.

Chaconne is a kind of Shangri-La, a rare and brave new world in the clouds, in which we are reminded, here above all, that ballet begins when Terpsichore touches Apollo's hand.

"Diamonds," from *Jewels*. Photo: Martha Swope

Karen Kain & Frank Augustyn

Most partnerships develop slowly and discreetly and gradually gain public recognition, but Karen Kain and Frank Augustyn of the National Ballet of Canada first really came together under the most gruelling, competitive, and public of occasions. Scarcely knowing each other and with only a few weeks rehearsal, the pair represented their country in the 1973 Moscow International Ballet Competition—and won. Against some of the best young dancers in the world, Kain and Augustyn triumphed in the pas de deux section, winning the coveted first prize. Kain remembers the experience with a combination of pleasure and dismay. "Russia was a gruelling experience for Frank and me," she said in an interview with Olga Maynard, "but well worth it. It was wonderful to dance at the Bolshoi Theatre, once we got accustomed to the raked stage! . . . But from a combination of nerves, and not knowing how to order food in restaurants, [we] lost so much weight that we were both terrified of losing our strength."

Considering that they were up against couples who had been practicing for nearly a year, she was astonished and delighted when they won. Of the three pas de deux they performed, one, the "Bluebird" pas de deux from *The Sleeping Beauty,* may have been something of a talisman, for it was in this that the couple first received critical attention. When the National Ballet of Canada had made its debut at the Metropolitan Opera House in New York in 1972, with Rudolf Nureyev, Kain and Augustyn dazzled audiences in the piece and immediately became talents to reckon with.

From the beginning of his association with the company, Nureyev had taken the two dancers under his wing. He chose Kain to be his first Aurora in *The Sleeping Beauty,* and Augustyn as his understudy in the role of Prince Florimund, as well as the Bluebird. As if

La Fille Mal Gardée. Photo: © 1977 Jack Vartoogian

"Nothing less than a solemn compact to become one entity."
—John Fraser

to support his instinct, Sol Hurok, that old hand at star-spotting, was attracted to them as well. In *Kain and Augustyn,* John Fraser tells the story of Hurok attending a company rehearsal at the Met and saying, "I've come to watch those two, they're stars you know, they're real stars." With New York and Moscow under their belts, Kain and Augustyn, at twenty-one and nineteen respectively, were well on their way.

Olga Maynard spotted a potential partnership very early. In her profile of Karen Kain, she wrote, "There seems to be an affinity between her and Augustyn . . . possibly they have the chemistry that may develop that rare blend of aesthetically satisfying and sensually provocative elements that make great pas de deux partners." As it happened, they did.

In many ways, the partnership of Kain and Augustyn resembles that of Antoinette Sibley and Anthony Dowell. John Fraser calls it "one of the few examples of total and felicitous equality." Like Sibley and Dowell, the two dancers came from the same school (modeled on the Royal Ballet School in England), have complementary physiques, and share a deep friendship. In an interview with Tobi Tobias, Kain even echoes Sibley and Dowell when

---

Duration of partnership: 1972–present
Company: The National Ballet of Canada
Principal Ballets: *Bayaderka, Coppélia, Le Corsaire, Giselle, La Fille Mal Gardée, Le Loup, The Sleeping Beauty, Swan Lake*

asked to analyze her relationship with Augustyn. "Physically we suit each other," she says. "Our lines melt together well, we hear music in the same way, we're equally strong-minded, and we're very good friends." Even before they came together, Augustyn was spotted by the National Ballet of Canada director Celia Franca as a possible partner for the unusually tall Kain. The two dancers are strong but refined technicians. During the company's first New York season, Rose Anne Thom commented on Augustyn's "clean line, strong elevation, and presence" and on Kain's sophistication and "strong and pure" dancing. What the couple had that was particularly their own, though, was a transparent classical style combined with a pert sensuality and an ebullient air of youth. Both have elegant, lithe bodies and slightly catlike faces, cheekbones drawn up, lips full. This combination of restraint and playfulness makes them delightful in something like *Coppélia* or Sir Frederick Ashton's *La Fille Mal Gardée,* a favorite work of both, which requires deft dancing, high spirits, and hints of ripe physical abandon. Reviewing a performance of the joyous but demanding Bournonville pas de deux from *Flower Festival in Genzano* (another such work), Leland Windreich wrote, "Their dancing flows like treacle. As far as technique is concerned, there's no challenge left for this pair but outer space." The high spirits are natural and in evidence off stage as well as on. Augustyn is a good storyteller, and Kain, in a rehearsal of *The Sleeping Beauty,* once awaited the awakening kiss of Florimund (Augustyn) wearing the wicked fairy Carabosse's wig, blue leg warmers, and horn-rimmed glasses. Their sensuality is a gift in the sultry showpiece pas de deux from *Le Corsaire* (made famous in the West by Nureyev and Fonteyn), where, whirling and leaping in gold lamé, Kain and Augustyn seem to glitter from within as well as without. And their innate classicism allows them to tackle confidently the difficult "Kingdom of the Shades" sequence from *La Bayadère* (called *Bayaderka* in the Canadian production), which in its removed purity of expression is like a dream of the perfect classical ballet style. Part of Kain and Augustyn's natural elegance is a real flair for costume. Clothes are never an afterthought. They transform and are transformed by them. Augustyn says that when he first saw himself in the Bluebird costume he thought it was someone else, and this sensation carried over into performance. "As the magnificent bird he literally hovers in the air," wrote Nancy Moore. "In preparing for flight, he holds his arms as if they were the folded wings of an eagle."

Another thing Kain and Augustyn have in common, aside from their temperament and

La Sylphide. Photo: © 1975 Linda Vartoogian

schooling, is the patronage of Rudolf Nureyev. For Augustyn, he was model as well as mentor. There is a striking physical resemblance between the two anyway, and you can see Nureyev's influence in Augustyn's assured and striking carriage on the stage. Nureyev's choice of Kain as a partner brought her international prominence, and the lessons she learned from him were implemented in her partnership with Augustyn to enhance their natural sympathy. "[Nureyev] taught me so much about dancing with—and to—a partner," Kain told Tobi Tobias, "how essential it is to relate, so that the audience can pick up that emotional excitement."

Kain and Augustyn are able to communicate their special relationship to the audience. According to Augustyn, their rapport is a product of conscious effort as well as unconscious affinity. "In performing we try to complement and communicate with each other in a way that will best realize for the audience a total expression. In so doing, a sensitivity and trust both physical and emotional have developed." As Olga Maynard puts it,

Bayaderka. Photo: MIRA

"Partnership in ballet is always a love affair," and Kain and Augustyn's efforts give their performances with each other special depth. In New York, they have been particularly praised in *Swan Lake*. "Frank . . . and I seem to have developed a very special rapport and in *Swan Lake* this is especially important," says Kain. "I get that extra bit of confidence about a performance when I know I will be dancing with him." Clive Barnes noticed this, and wrote in one review, "Miss Kain's Odette-Odile is well known to New York, but she has never danced it with the power, beauty and authority that she brought to the dual role . . . [her] heavy-lidded, langorous Odette, with its soft caressive arms, found its counterpart in her flashing, confidently aggressive Odile." And he found Augustyn, whose long line makes bowing as eloquent as dancing, "in his acting and in his dancing . . . every inch the prince." Frances Herridge agreed. "Last night's cast had Frank Augustyn as a truly noble prince and Karen Kain as its

superb Odette-Odile . . . his elevation is admirable, his transitions smooth, and his bearing flawless . . . Miss Kain always had a sure balance and clean line, but now she has added a shimmering radiance and soft suppleness to her White Swan. And her Black Swan has impressive authority."

The pair brings an air of youth and poignancy to another favorite, *Giselle* (it was the first ballet Kain ever saw), and during the National Ballet of Canada's 1976 season in New York they were given one performance of it together—an outstanding one—in the otherwise Nureyev-dominated engagement. They were also invited to dance *Giselle* with the Bolshoi, a rare honor for western dancers. While in Russia, they took Asaf Messerer's class with such Russian greats as Maya Plisetskaya, Ekaterina Maximova, and Vladimir Vasiliev. Natalia Bessmertnova and Leonid Lavrovsky came especially to teach them the Bolshoi version of the mime scene, and once

again, as at the International Ballet Competition, the two dancers more than held their own in Russia.

In their performances of the classics, Kain and Augustyn are respectful but dynamic and manage, as John Fraser notes, to be unaffected but compelling. "Their dancing style has remained remarkably uncluttered with affectations, and this sincere, unstudied, and totally refreshing approach makes most of their performances of the classics seem newly minted." At the same time, they are interested in modern works and have danced in such pieces as John Cranko's *Romeo and Juliet,* Roland Petit's *Le Loup,* and various works choreographed by colleagues at the National Ballet of Canada. These include a *Rite of Spring* by Constantin Patsalas, which showed that their elegant line could express primitive passion.

In all of these pieces they displayed, as John Fraser writes, "nothing less than a solemn compact to become one entity." This entity soon built upon its early successes to receive wide acclaim, especially in Canada, where the pair were deluged with offers for guest appearances and television shows. They were heroes in their own country and pioneers in the National Ballet of Canada, where they heralded a new, more emotional style of dancing in the sometimes phlegmatic company. By 1978, Gina Mallet could write, in *Dance in Canada* magazine, "The Kain/Augustyn partnership cannot yet be matched [in the National Ballet]. It works seamlessly . . . Karen Kain and Frank Augustyn are demi-gods. Their very appearance sets off an ovation."

They are still dancers—and legends—in the making, but already they have created a firm place for themselves in dance history. Commenting on their relationship, Augustyn said, "There are certain times and certain people that seem predestined in one's life and upon reflecting one cannot contemplate any other in their place. Karen holds such a place in my life." And the Kain-Augustyn partnership already holds such a place in the world of dance.

Swan Lake. Photo: MIRA

Ekaterina Maximova & Vladimir Vasiliev

Duration of partnership: 1962–present
Companies: Bolshoi Ballet, guest appearances at Nervi Festival and with the Maly Ballet among others
Principal Ballets: *Don Quixote, Giselle, The Nutcracker, Spartacus, The Stone Flower*

Don Quixote. Photo: Courtesy of *Dancing Times*

While some marriages are made in heaven, others are made in Varna. The 1964 International Ballet Competition really marked the beginning of the partnership between Ekaterina Maximova and Vladimir Vasiliev, a partnership that later included marriage. Maximova was awarded a gold medal, and Vasiliev won the coveted, but rarely given, Grand Prix. A film of the competition shows the pair dancing a dazzling and confident *Don Quixote* pas de deux—clean, bold, and so self-sufficient that Maximova was able to perform the arduous thirty-two fouettés with her hands on her hips. The full-length ballet, which combines technical audacity with warm characterization, became one of this couple's signature pieces.

Varna set the seal on reputations that had

**"Here is a rare couple whose talents complete each other with one accord, reaching an exceptional quality."
—Marie-Françoise Christout**

been in the making since 1957, when Elena Bocharnikova, then director of the Bolshoi School, boasted to Arnold Haskell of Maximova and Vasiliev as her prize pupils. While very young, they were among the dancers on the Bolshoi's first tour in New York in 1959. John Martin noticed their spectacular work in *The Flames of Paris,* and *Time* magazine did thumbnail sketches of them. Maximova: "She displays a beautifully limpid line of movement, effortless control and more bubbly, fresh faced charm than any other member of the

The Nutcracker. Photo: Courtesy of *Dancing Times*

company." Vasiliev: "A favorite trick: to bound straight off the stage, extend one leg, tuck the other under him and casually descend in perfect balance on one foot." In 1962 they were back again, on a tour headed by Maya Plisetskaya, and although they did not dance together, they attracted attention individually. Vasiliev had already created the virile and heroic title role in Yuri Grigorovich's *Spartacus* and was much acclaimed in this, while Maximova was making her mark in *Giselle*. "Maximova is a wonderful dancer, and already a wonderful Giselle," wrote Lillian Moore. "There is little doubt that in a few years' time she will be a great one."

The following year, the pair were in London with the company, where Richard Buckle saw them in *Paganini*. He thought Maximova "lovely" and noted Vasiliev's chief quality as a performer. "[He] dances superbly and gives everything emotionally at the same time."

In 1964 came Varna (Vasiliev also won the Prix Nijinsky in this year) and the beginning of a long international career which has included tours throughout Europe and in America.

Maximova was the chosen successor of the Bolshoi's great prima ballerina, Galina Ulanova. Ulanova's lyrical style, a product of the more refined and expressive Kirov school, was imparted to Maximova when the older dancer coached her in *Giselle*. Maximova's spare delicacy made her the perfect Giselle, but she had also been schooled in the bolder and more vigorous Bolshoi style, whose exemplar was Maya Plisetskaya. The frail frame disguised a steely technique and an open, irrepressible quality which made her ideal, also, for the very different role of Kitri the innkeeper's daughter in *Don Quixote*. In a review of a Bolshoi tour of the English provinces, Clive Barnes celebrated her versatility. "What a fantastic dancer this Maximova is! Witty, vibrant, charming, delicate, mercurial, even, in a wry way, tragic—you name it, and Miss Maximova has it."

If Maximova received the balletic mantle from Ulanova, Vasiliev seems to have been born with one from Nijinsky, as Peter Williams was unafraid to point out in a review of *Don Quixote*. "His dancing all through is spectacular, but in the last act duet he danced the most incredible solo I have ever seen from any male dancer. He even managed to give the appearance of being suspended in the air, something which we have always been told was only achieved by Nijinsky."

But in addition to his phenomenal prowess, Vasiliev has a quality described by John Percival simply as "humanity," which he defined as "the ability to embody the generosity of spirit and understanding that are man's highest qualities to illuminate the dance, and to use the dance to enrich life." The fierce and exuberant technician is, as well, a great actor, able to express and project a complex range of feelings—tenderness, pity, grief, joy—and, of course, like all great humanitarians, he has the gift of comedy. His high leaps, his mane of blond hair, make him seem godlike, but he expresses man's soul. In Vasiliev, the lion has indeed lain down with the lamb.

Maximova, too, has some of this warmth and range of soul, and their performances together seem organic, with the characters growing and changing before our eyes. This is particularly true of *Giselle,* with its two worlds. Vasiliev had partnered Ulanova in one of her last appearances (in *Chopiniana*) and this may have made him even more receptive to Maximova in this lyrical, romantic mode. Maximova, in turn, seems like a bud opening to the sun. "It is beautiful," reported Peter Williams, "the way her trust in Albrecht gradually overcomes her gaucheness; this makes her final realization of the deception all the more heart-rending." In her mad scene, the real and the spirit world seem to overlap in her. "As it becomes more phantasmagoric she gradually takes on the mantle of the wili that she is to become." Vasiliev's Albrecht, too, invites analysis in terms of drama: "One is aware of a person who, although his attachment to Giselle may have at first been a passing flutter, is conscious of a deeper love growing all the time. The subtlety with which Vasiliev suggests this, mainly through facial expression, is in line with great theatre actors." But acting and dancing are inseparable for these two. "From the acting point of view," Williams continued, "it appears as if both Maximova and Vasiliev had studied with the Moscow Art Theatre; from the dancing aspect they could have come from nowhere other than the Bolshoi. Both were as near to perfection as I ever hope to see."

Two years later, in France, where the couple was guesting with the Maly Ballet, Marie-Françoise Christout saw not only an exceptional performance of *Giselle,* but an expression of their unity. "Ekaterina Maximova has never, I think, shown such completeness," she wrote, "as much in the first act, where she seemed more innocent and guileless than ever, as in the second, where she proved both lyrical and dramatic within her icy unreality. In Vladimir Vasiliev she clearly finds the ideal partner, attentive, gifted, with princely authority. In the second act particularly he is not afraid to 'dance' his grief in an entirely personal and startling way, throwing himself into flashing leaps in the paroxysm of despair. Here is a rare couple whose talents complete and deepen each other with one accord, reaching an exceptional quality."

The couple are able to achieve the same

Spartacus. Photo: Courtesy of *Dancing Times*

accord and quality even in dramatically slighter works. Like *Giselle, The Nutcracker* requires dancing on two levels. It contains some beautiful examples of pure Russian classicism, but every step for the girl and her Prince must have the delicate pearly sheen of a childhood fantasy. The charm and vivacity that had attracted people to Maximova from her earliest performances served her well in this ballet, and Vasiliev as the Prince combined impeccable demeanor with incredible dancing. After an early performance in New York, Clive Barnes reported, "Ekaterina Maximova as Marie was all snowflake fragility and innocent beguilement, and she even managed the torturous turns given her in the pas de deux with a smiling and sensitive aplomb. As her prince, Vladimir Vasiliev radiated nobility and purity, qualities also justly descriptive of his electric dancing." Eight years later, they were still enchanting Kathrine Sorley Walker. "As an actress she [Maximova] has the rare gift of total expressiveness in face and gesture. . . . Her partnership with Vladimir Vasiliev, particularly in the long and hard-to-sustain ecstatic mood of the transformation dancing, had the resource and brilliance of great doubles play on center court, where well-balanced abilities and exciting co-operation gain championship points."

Both histrionic and athletic abilities are called for in typical Bolshoi repertory pieces like Grigorovich's *The Stone Flower* and *Spartacus.* Maximova and Vasiliev excelled at both. The role of Katerina, the heroine of *The Stone Flower*, was Maximova's first after leaving school. The lyrical delicacy and piquancy that make her a beautiful Giselle were used to convey the innocence and trust of a young girl, but Katerina expresses her emotions on a grand scale, and her hopes and fears, as she eludes the lustful land baron and tries to rescue her lover from the bewitching Mistress of the Copper Mountain, are communicated in soaring lifts and leaps. Vasiliev was the idealistic Danila. "Lovely little Miss Maximova . . . is enough to melt the heart of any witch, however cruel," wrote John Martin. "She has an exquisite dancer's body, capable of virtually any movement required of it and of making it seem to flow spontaneously out of simple emotional conviction. Beautiful to look at, with a radiant smile and a childish guilelessness, she is the ideal of all the young sweethearts of the story books. Vladimir Vasiliev was . . . the winning young hero, dancing like an engaging whirlwind."

Poignant expressiveness is also the key to the role of Phrygia, Spartacus's faithful wife. Peter Williams said she had "all the right melting uxorious quality," and Richard Buckle that her "whole body brimmed with love and idealism." The object of this, who, as a character and as a dancer took sustenance from her, was Vasiliev in one of his greatest roles, a quintessential one. Fierce and powerful dancing expresses courage and humanity heightened to the stuff of legend. In his revolt against the dictator Crassus, Spartacus stands for mankind fighting its oppressors, and no one who saw Vasiliev could forget him. "No praise can be too high," wrote Richard Buckle. "His glorious technique is at the service of his expression." In France, Marie-Françoise Christout found that he "outdid himself in the strength, virtuosity and passion, not to mention technical virtuosity in the title role." And Maximova "was again a moving Phrygia." To Peter Williams, he seemed both man and symbol. "Vasiliev has now burnished his Spartacus . . . to the point where it shines out brilliantly in a murky Roman world." In 1970, Vasiliev was awarded the Lenin Prize, one of the Soviet Union's highest honors, for this role.

The organic quality of Maximova-Vasiliev performances comes partly from their flexibility as actors. In company with a limited repertory and rigid traditions, like the Bolshoi, it would be easy to become petrified, but when Vasiliev referred once to the importance of remembering, indeed, the danger of forgetting "dramatic art," he implied the couple's willingness to absorb the ideals of others and utilize their own experience. As John Percival wrote, "They still dance in the true Bolshoi style as we remember it of old. But they have watched carefully the ideas of others and taken from these whatever could be used to enhance their own concept."

"The true Bolshoi style" combines well with freedom in characterization in *Don Quixote,* which brought down on Maximova and Vasiliev's heads a rain of ecstatic superlatives from critics. A French newspaper conveyed some of the couple's playfulness when it published a photograph of them at poolside in Monte Carlo, improvising a spectacular one-arm lift with Maximova suspended perpendicularly over Vasiliev's head and grinning. The accompanying caption read, "Ils sont deux qui accumulent le charme, la beauté, la technique, le talent et la gentillesse." (Roughly, "These two have charm, beauty, technique, talent, and refinement.") Just this sort of daring, ease, and amusement is called for in *Don Quixote* and Maximova and Vasiliev are unforgettable. "A spectacle not to be missed," insisted Clive Barnes. "They surpassed themselves," wrote Irène Lidova from Paris. "She, in wonderful form, lively, alluring. He, marvelously humorous and elegant, light and charming—they provoked an explosive response in the house; small bouquets showered the stage, and the couple took countless curtain calls." Even when they performed only the Grand Pas de Deux, as at Varna, Richard Buckle, no fan of the extract, wrote, "Maximova and Vasiliev danced like a dream. . . . No dancing could be more spectacular"; but when they appeared in the full-length ballet, they created a whole world. "In the face of their performances, everything else melts into a noonday Barcelona haze," wrote Peter Williams. "Maximova is naughty, flirtatious and thoroughly adorable; her come-on/keep your distance affair with Basilio almost becomes a question of 'anything you can do, I can do better,' a lively competition as they soar higher and longer, turn faster and faster.

"Maximova is a . . . natural Kitri, in line with the contemporary practice of bringing out the human qualities of the part. . . . Vasiliev brings out the rough humor of the part . . . and the play of emotions over his face, the way he uses his shoulders and hands subtly conveys to the audience everything that is passing through his mind."

Now, fifteen years after their triumph at Varna, Maximova and Vasiliev are still working together, though they are no longer married. "The great dancer," wrote John Percival, "must be able to hold his own in virtuosity with those who make virtuosity their chief virtue, but he brings something else to his work, something more moving and rewarding." This is true of great partnerships as well, and it is this "something" that Maximova and Vasiliev have given us.

Gelsey Kirkland & Mikhail Baryshnikov

"They dance at full height."
—Arlene Croce

When Mikhail Baryshnikov defected from the USSR in 1974, the dance world, which knew him to be the most exciting thing in male dancing since Nureyev and possibly its greatest technician, was ready to give him anything he wanted. What he wanted, almost immediately, was a chance to dance with Gelsey Kirkland. She had gone to see him dance in Toronto, not long after his defection, and they had met at a supper party following his performance. With typical Russian directness, he reportedly murmured, "Good partner, right size." A few days later, Kirkland received a phone call inviting her to be his partner. "Well, I just flipped out," she remembers. "I just flipped. I remember screaming at the top of my voice, 'What do you mean, *would* I dance with him? Of course, I will.'" There was something fairy tale-like about a partnership beginning this way—a prince choosing his lady without the interference of ugly sisters or the benefit of glass slippers. As Robert Garis observed, "It is a very Hollywood thing, this great dancer defects and he says that the person he wants to dance with is Gelsey Kirkland. It is almost irresistible."

Kirkland and Baryshnikov had seen each other dance when the New York City Ballet, with which she was then a principal, toured Russia. The young Kirkland, daring and delicate, was the latest of George Balanchine's prodigies, and Baryshnikov saw her dance the demanding *Theme and Variations.* She, in turn, got an opportunity to watch him in class. "He was such a tremendous inspiration," she recalled. "I had never seen such dancing, such power." When they came together, they represented the highest forms of two different dance styles, styles which were, in fact, two branches of the same family. The Russian classical tradition continued in Russia when the Maryinsky evolved into the Kirov Ballet, and it was recreated in America by George Balanchine. Robert Greskovic has called the Kirkland-Baryshnikov partnership "the meeting of two of our dance world's greatest legacies." It was balletic détente.

Kirkland and Baryshnikov first appeared together as guests with the Royal Winnipeg Ballet. An advance article by John Fraser called the performance "the world debut of a new partnership." And so it proved to be. Soon after, Baryshnikov was offered a contract by American Ballet Theatre, and Kirkland left the New York City Ballet to join him there.

They had a good deal to offer one another. Kirkland had always wanted to dance dramatic roles, and Baryshnikov was the catalyst that made it possible. He, on the other hand, idolized George Balanchine and was eager to dance in his ballets. They both got their chance. American Ballet Theatre revived its production of Balanchine's *Theme and Variations,* and Baryshnikov squired Kirkland through her triumphant debut as Giselle.

Baryshnikov, at first, had difficulties with Balanchine's angled, distorted, and rapid-fire style, but in *Baryshnikov at Work,* he credits much of what he learned about *Theme* to Kirkland. "When I first danced this part I learned a tremendous amount from watching Gelsey, because she knows so well how to pace the ballet. She had learned how to create this marvelous atmosphere of reserve, of harmony, and at the same time to project the clarity and brilliance, the fireworks." He soon came into his own in this work, with Arlene Croce praising his "quick attack, compact delivery and delicacy." The ballerina role she called "Aurora re-written in lightning," and when fleet and radiant Kirkland joined with Baryshnikov, *The Sleeping Beauty* truly entered the modern age.

The first big triumph of their partnership was *Giselle.* Baryshnikov had danced the role of Albrecht before and was already famous for his extraordinary *brisés volés* and other unequaled feats of technique in the second act, but in Kirkland he found the perfect foil for his sincere and ardent characterization. And Kirkland, fragile, wide-eyed, transparently light on her feet, found the ballet for which she might have been born. "The perfect apposition of a star and role," as Arlene Croce wrote. George

Duration of partnership: 1974–present
Company: American Ballet Theatre
Principal Ballets: *La Bayadère, Coppélia, Don Quixote, Giselle, The Nutcracker, Theme and Variations*

Don Quixote. Photo: Martha Swope

Gelles agreed and wrote that Kirkland "was vastly helped by her partner, Mr. Baryshnikov, who for once was taking a back seat and apparently enjoying it. Miss Kirkland's triumph was also his, and they went beautifully well together." Robert Jacobson analyzed their quality: "[Baryshnikov's] commitment to the emotional details of the part is extraordinary, and with Miss Kirkland he shares a heartbreaking vulnerability, ravishing lyric purity and thrilling bursts of energy." "A perfect pair of lovers," stated Frances Herridge. Walter Terry was rhapsodic. "Miss Kirkland, fragile in appearance, and steel-strong technically, is one of the best Giselles to be found. Baryshnikov is, in many ways (aesthetically as well as in spectacular virtuosities) one of the great dance artists of the age. How marvelous!—What an honor!—to have them, to see them, to cherish their dancing together." To Croce, it was "a promise fulfilled," and a gossip column reported that the pair "tore

Theme and Variations. Photo: Beverley Gallegos

down the house."

Kirkland-Baryshnikov performances frequently ravish the viewer with detail. Their technique is so pure and clear that the slightest preparation or angle of the body suddenly becomes terribly exciting. They make deliberation as exciting as other people make speed—and then deliver the speed as well. Watching them is like watching classicism in close-up, as if a master cameraman is directing their performances. But their technical perfection is never chilly. It can be daring, playful, or lyrical and tender. This accounts for their success in the "Kingdom of the Shades" sequence from *La Bayadère*. When the haunted Solor dances with the spirit of his dead love, Nikiya, the pas de deux requires the utmost in classical perfection while conveying passion and melancholy. Reviewing Baryshnikov's performance, Robert Greskovic asked, "Was Kirkland the Nikiya he's been searching for ever since he first danced this Kirov role some years before?" and concluded, "He danced like she was. She danced like she knew it." The pair can also turn technical brilliance up full strength, as they did in the virtuoso blockbuster pas de deux from *Le Corsaire,* which they performed at American Ballet Theatre's thirty-fifth anniversary gala. "The company's newest acquisitions . . . were there to knock 'em dead in the aisles," reported Walter Terry.

Impeccable technique can be awesome and distant, but Kirkland and Baryshnikov's other side is an endearing, piquant ragamuffin quality, which lets them be vulnerable and playful on the stage (when Clive Barnes wrote that they danced "as if they had grown up together," this was the quality he was appreciating) and makes them perfect for comedies like *La Fille Mal Gardée* and *Coppélia,* which next entered their repertory.

The essence of comedy is the natural and harmonious resolution of difficulties, and this is the essence of Kirkland and Baryshnikov's dancing. They are buoyant but tender. Anna Kisselgoff reported that in *Fille,* Baryshnikov, with Kirkland, was "a gentler, more romantic Colin who was every inch as gallant as he should be. Certainly he was the perfect match for the Lise whose sweetness Miss Kirkland conveyed so appealingly." Nancy Goldner wrote, "Kirkland and Baryshnikov's innocence, combined with their impeccable dance styles, rendered them children of paradise."

They are equally successful in the sprightly *Coppélia,* which combines slapstick humor with demanding classical passages. In the pas de deux, they are perfectly attuned; even their flourishes are the same. "They dance at full height, so to speak," wrote Arlene Croce. To Alan Kriegsman, it was a symbol of their versatility. "As the promise of their partnership unfolds into reality, its limits seem to recede to infinity."

At the end of their first season together, George Gelles informed readers that Kirkland and Baryshnikov were "the most promising partnership since blinis and caviar." Bill Zakariasen less reverently called them "the Laurel and Hardy of ballet." It seemed inevitable that when Baryshnikov began to do his own staging of ballets, Kirkland should be his instrument. In 1976 he mounted a production of *The Nutcracker* for American Ballet Theatre. The role of Clara, the child who is led into womanhood by the Prince, is a perfect one for Kirkland, and Baryshnikov, as the Prince, makes classical decorum an emotional excitement. Analyzing the role, Kirkland said, "Clara's dream-relationship to the Prince; it's not a big romantic vision. It's the very first experience, that opens up a whole new world." This sense of discovery and enchantment is transmitted to the audience. "Her dancing had a delicacy and perfection of placement that was a joy to watch," remarked Clive Barnes. "Mr. Baryshnikov . . . partnered her with lithe gallantry. He makes the cavalier very dashing and radiant, like a knight in shining ardor." "Much of the joyfulness of Clara and the prince's relationship is transmitted in their frequent passages of unison dancing," wrote Anna Kisselgoff. Tobi Tobias called the pas de deux "dreams of Baryshnikovian classicism, full of a fierce energy that is made to look angelic." She noted that he and Kirkland had the same gift "for achieving clarity and softness simultaneously." Their gift for bringing out details is emotional as well as technical, and makes possible what Kirkland calls "the vividness of immediate things." Their childlike quality helped convey the mood of the ballet. Neither dancer has classically elegant looks. Kirkland has a tiny, coltlike body and large head. She has been compared to a raccoon. Baryshnikov is compact, has unruly blond hair and boyish, mobile features. In romances, they seem particularly grave and innocent; in comedies, irrepressibly ebullient. Their elegance is all in style and placement.

Baryshnikov's next production, *Don Quixote,* showed the pair in a different light. The barber Basil and the innkeeper's daughter Kitri combine brassy flirtation with passages of virtuoso athletic dancing. It is an all-out ballet, and no one had ever before seen them dancing at quite that pitch. Kirkland, especially, was fast developing a reputation as a romantic ballerina, and she astonished people as a bundle of highflying temperament. "That girl doesn't stop," said Kirkland of Kitri. Together, they struck sparks. "Baryshnikov was flying and flowing," reported Clive Barnes. "Not only did he dance like a fire cracker who has found a fire, he also acted with quite extraordinary brilliance . . . you watch Miss Kirkland and you receive an insight about what dancing is all about. . . . You are in the presence of greatness. It is as bewilderingly simple as that." "The ideal partner," Baryshnikov has told John Gruen, "is one with whom you can dance with your eyes closed." In the pas de deux, with their daring leaps and lifts that almost defy gravity, Kirkland and Baryshnikov give off an air of supreme confidence. "In their duets she and Baryshnikov—both exquisitely centered dancers—can exploit a crazy daring," wrote Tobi Tobias. . . . "They treat treacherous stretches of empty space as if the air were cushioned."

Daring is at the center of the partnership. In their security, they are able to experiment with their medium. They are perfectionists who go beyond perfection to invention. Marcia Siegel observes, "They both excel in the fine details of classicism—precision in footwork, musicality, elegance of line, and a certain cold dance intelligence compounded of security, imagination and daring, that allows the great performers to decide how they're going to do something while they're doing it. . . . They're both very reticent dancers . . . But inside both of them is a kind of rage that will suddenly launch them into the most dangerous gambles, impossible leaps, precarious balances, delays of the inevitable." The two dancers appreciate each other's inexhaustible versatility. Asked about Kirkland, Baryshnikov said, "She is a first-class ballerina. I think her dance personality can be many-sided. She can be dramatic, she is excellent in so many styles. There are so many roles in which our personalities mesh well." "Misha is an inspiration," said Kirkland, "in the sense that he goes even beyond his potential as a dancer. He's so totally daring that the energy level feeds your energy." And she told *Vogue,* "With Misha, you realize how limitless the human body can be. He's shown us another vocabulary for the next generation."

Kirkland and Baryshnikov are like diamonds—multifaceted, perfect surfaces containing a hidden flame within. (Baryshnikov even called Kirkland "a diamond . . . who could fit into any setting.") The polished surface is their style, and the flame is the emotion that illuminates it. With stylists like these, steps become, rather than indicate, forms of feeling. "Every impulse, every movement must be sincere," Baryshnikov has said. And reviewing their *Giselle,* Frances Herridge wrote, "There are no dead spots on stage with merely moving bodies. The drama between them is unending, enthralling, immensely moving . . . they dance the difficult choreography as though still acting." Arlene Croce observed, "The dancing pours out of the mime as if in a fever of pent-up eloquence." In Kirkland's words, the partnership is "a spiritual relationship. Feelings flow back and forth."

Offstage, not all the feelings have been harmonious, for emotional and intellectual reasons. The two dancers had a brief romance, and its end caused some tension between them, but most of their difficulties in rehearsals have been because they represent two different approaches to performing. Kirkland is an inexhaustible analyst. Baryshnikov, though he has done more than any other male dancer to extend the range of his movements, works by instinct. Kirkland has described their work relationship candidly, "If we can get past the fights, we have a rapport that really works. Oddly enough, we have trouble working together, because we have very separate approaches to work. He has no patience at all, and I have a lot of patience. I like to analyze everything, and he just wants to do it and leave. And really, we're totally different

La Fille Mal Gardée. Photo: Martha Swope

the most literal sense, unforgettable. Not only the mood they create, but also each movement, is a distinct and memorable image. In a review of *Don Quixote*, Deborah Jowitt wrote, "[Kirkland] and Baryshnikov, together and separately, are the kinds of dancers who can make you construe dancing in ways you never thought about. In the final pas de deux, when Kitri turns alone with one leg out to the side, then twists into arabesque as Basil steps in to hold her, they show you a brave independent statement that becomes a mutual endeavor and curves into an embrace." It is, in a way, the perfect description of dynamic but traditional, impeccably controlled but daring, union; "a brave independent statement that becomes a mutual endeavor."

The Nutcracker. Photo: Beverley Gallegos

dancers—but *completely*. What seems to work is the contrast, and I think the rapport we have will always be special."

But when *Vogue* described the partnership as "electric, mysterious, sadly sweet . . . a magical coming together of instinct-fired emotion and of finely honed technique," it was observing the way their differences were resolved onstage.

At the time of this writing, the Kirkland-Baryshnikov partnership is in a transitional period. She has had several debilitating illnesses, interrupting her career, and has just returned to the stage. He is back at American Ballet Theatre as artistic director as well as principal dancer after a year with the New York City Ballet. It is to be hoped that the future will include the two of them, because they are, in

Giselle. Photo: Martha Swope

Nadezhda Pavlova & Vyacheslav Gordeyev

"The Pavlova/Gordeyev partnership seems made in Terpsichore's heaven."
—Robert Greskovic

"Slava means 'glory' in Russian, Nadya, 'hope.' One might call this company The Band of Hope and Glory." John Simon was reviewing the 1979 Bolshoi Ballet season in New York, but referring particularly to the sensational performances given by Nadezhda Pavlova and Vyacheslav Gordeyev.

The two young dancers, who are man and wife as well as partners, are among the most glorious ever seen, and for the Bolshoi they certainly represent the hope of—if not the look of—the future.

In 1973, just a few weeks after Pavlova had won the Grand Prix and Gordeyev a gold medal at the Moscow International Ballet Competition (the Soviet magazine *Culture and Life* featured them on the cover), the two dancers made a fantastically successful American debut. Gordeyev, at twenty-four, appeared to be the apotheosis of classical style, with a breathtaking elegance and precision rare in Bolshoi *danseurs.* Pavlova, at seventeen, was a genuine prodigy, whose phenomenal gifts went beyond formal perfection. She seemed to extend and redefine the classical vocabulary while she performed it.

Wilfried Hofmann, who saw her in Vienna with her then company, the Perm Ballet, wrote, "She moves like someone who was born into this medium, and as a genius at that." In America, critics were eager to analyze the range of that genius. "The Bolshoi's newest star . . . doesn't resemble her namesake," wrote Arlene Croce, "and she doesn't resemble any other dancer I've seen. At seventeen, she is an authentic original; she shows you the full grandeur of the style of classical dancing she has been trained in and, at the same time, the fullness of her own contribution to it. . . . Pavlova is the mistress of what she does, and she touched me in innumerable ways—most of

all in the sweet unconcern with which she did the undoable."

At seventeen, Pavlova was coltish, with legs so long and hips so articulate they seemed almost freakish. "The undoable" included inexhaustible jumps and what Croce called "high-voltage arcs"—those sweeping extensions of almost 180°. She combined this pile-driver technique with an almost Victorian reticence and delicacy of manner that could bubble over into gaiety, when her large eyes shone and her grave little face was split with a grin. It was as if Plisetskaya had been sheathed in Fonteyn. As Robert Greskovic described her: "Her legs glare from her hips with white-hot energy; they're like newly forged steel, setting, cooling, and workable. . . . Posé arabesque with upstretched arms and spine was a moment of dance/music glory for both Pavlova and her audience. Together we forgot the child and reveled in the dance." In pas de bourrée, skittering along the floor on pointe, "she seemed almost to be giggling aloud."

Gordeyev was the ideal partner for this astonishing girl. "He must be one of the best male classical dancers in the world," said Croce. Robert Greskovic elaborated, "He does everything in the classical vocabulary and does it one unit better and more. He has a silken plié, a sustained and sky-high elevation, and smooth clean finishes . . . he is in the first hour of the coming of age." Like Pavlova, he seemed to have been born into his medium, which he deployed with a naturalness that was almost casual, but a finish that was purely classical. As Tobi Tobias would write in a later profile, "Gordeyev is an anomaly. He looks like a character dancer, moves like a classical dancer, and is well on his way to proving himself one of the finest of his young generation. Startlingly, he's *there* onstage, with a suddenness of being in motion and a purity of shape in space. . . . He moves through classical enchainements with the born-to-it naturalness of ghetto children dancing in New York's hot summer streets."

Their performances in 1973 were with a special "Stars of the Bolshoi Ballet" touring group, which did not present any full-length ballets. Audiences saw Pavlova and Gordeyev in the pas de deux from *The Nutcracker* and *La*

Duration of partnership: 1973, 1975–present
Company: Bolshoi Ballet
Principal Ballets: *La Fille Mal Gardée, Giselle, The Legend of Love, The Nutcracker, Romeo and Juliet, Spartacus*

La Fille Mal Gardée pas de deux. Photo: MIRA

Fille Mal Gardée, and in each, pristinely classical or crisply bucolic, they enchanted. Clive Barnes called their *Nutcracker* "an exemplary demonstration of the art of pas de deux" and said that *Fille* "invariably brought the house down, rapturously performed as it was." Their rapport with one another seemed to be the result of security and high spirits, rather than dramatic pose. Gordeyev was the perfect gallant partner, not in that he remained an unobtrusive porter, but in that his own dazzling embellishments seemed directed toward his ballerina. Arlene Croce saw this as a reflection of his relationship to his art. "Gordeyev's dancing, both when he is a partner and when he is a soloist, is full of those grace notes that weaker technicians leave out . . . those little extras of his seem to come from inside, as tokens of an ardent sincerity toward his ballerina, his public, and the art of dancing." In a photograph of the *Fille* pas de deux, we can see the partnership frozen at the height of the action. Pavlova's sweeping, athletic, almost vertical penchée arabesque is softened by her sweet smile and the way her head tilts confidingly toward Gordeyev's outstretched arm. He is holding a flawless fourth position, but the supple curve of his body is toward her, and he is smiling lovingly and admiringly. For dancers like these, character is not trowelled on, but revealed by style—that much more crystalline for *Nutcracker,* more broad for *Fille.* "She is pizzicato Sugar Plum and country-green Lise. He *is* Nutcracker turned glittering Prince, and boyish, brave Colas," declared Robert Greskovic. "When Pavlova prepared to rush toward her prince/beau, Gordeyev simultaneously readied himself to receive his princess/belle with open arms and respondent confidence."

Romeo and Juliet. Photo: MIRA

After the golden pair's return to Russia, Pavlova danced for a year with the Perm Ballet. In June of 1975, she joined the Bolshoi, and on one memorable day, 6 November 1975, celebrated with Gordeyev her official debut as a soloist with the company, her official debut in *Giselle,* and her marriage. At the wedding, Pavlova wore a long white lace dress and a tall headdress. Gordeyev looked like a grandee in a stiff white dress shirt with an enormous bow tie. Three hours later, it was tulle and velvet at the Bolshoi, and Natalia Roslavleva reported the event to the *Dancing Times.* As Giselle, Pavlova showed "a truly extraordinary extension, lightness of jump, lovely line in arabesque, and a true exhilaration that makes her dance as a bird sings." In the second act, her power channeled into a feathery lightness, Roslavleva "believed she was a wili, a daughter of the air, and that Vyacheslav Gordeyev . . . was merely trying to hold her

with his arms so that she would not take wing and fly away." The couple received numerous ovations, and the curtain calls were as lavish as a second wedding. "The audience loved Nadia and her partner . . . and cheered themselves hoarse. Nadia was given huge bouquets of white roses with white ribbons. Gordeyev received flowers with pink ribbons but he handed them all to his ballerina, whose arms were so full she could hardly hold them."

Pavlova did not join the 1975 Bolshoi tour to New York. Gordeyev did and was interviewed by Tobi Tobias, who commented on his combination of restraint and buoyancy, of casualness and aristocratic grandeur. "He looks like the boy down the block, who somehow just happens to be a prince." Gordeyev said he felt that each role was "fascinating in its own way," and that he read literature related to his parts. But this intellectual approach is enhanced by innate

The Nutcracker pas de deux. Photo: MIRA

qualities: "Every individual, by his physical 'given' and his own emotional qualities, is unique, and this is what you bring to the role that no other person can bring." A strong believer in Russian heritage, he asserted that "there is no Russian who doesn't like poetry," which may be what gives them an edge in the fantastical world of ballet.

In 1979, the Bolshoi was back in America, and for the first time audiences were able to see Pavlova and Gordeyev in full-length roles. Pavlova had matured, growing into her long legs, and was an intriguing blend of girlishness and womanliness, innocence, and sensuality. Gordeyev's noble clarity of style made the broadly heroic Bolshoi pieces seem more finished than usual. "The beauty and power are still there," wrote Croce, "brighter and steadier than before." Because of their popularity, the couple had starring roles in three of the five ballets presented by the company: *Spartacus, Romeo and Juliet,* and *The Legend of Love,* a steamy story of sister rivals with a Turkish setting.

Pavlova and Gordeyev's ability to make style into drama was apparent everywhere. Of *Spartacus,* Anna Kisselgoff wrote, "Miss Pavlova is a unique dancer. No other ballerina has such a swivel-smooth leg extension and can combine this supple acrobatic body with a lyric charm that goes straight to the heart. It was the rapport established by Miss Pavlova and Mr. Gordeyev that made every movement so dramatic. Often it was merely a question of timing . . . the leave-taking in Act III was turned into the most eloquent exploration of a tender relationship . . . very suddenly the image of Miss Pavlova held upside down in a one-arm lift . . . became a symbol of ecstatic love." "What fantastic dancers they are," cried Clive Barnes. Arlene Croce noted again Gordeyev's "class" as a classicist: "the mood of quiet elegance with which he sustains technical feats," and the way technical ease and dramatic sincerity are equated in his performances. "Gordeyev reminds me of Martha Graham's phrase 'divine normal.' He has strength, virile beauty, perfection of style, and also the gift of appearing utterly genuine on the stage. . . . Classical dancing is a language he speaks naturally."

The Bolshoi's new production of *Romeo and Juliet,* by Yuri Grigorovich, is bland and bloodless, but Pavlova and Gordeyev were poignant as the young lovers, and she was a beautiful figure, with her flat, stark face, all emotion held in reserve above the great flame-colored dress. But it was in *The Legend of Love,* a silly ballet, but with tremendous opportunities for dancing, that the pair really came into their own. "[Gordeyev] did display again and again that well remembered catapulting grand jeté of his, and frequently Pavlova was there leaping at his side, as loftily, as hungrily, as tirelessly as he," wrote Croce. She continued, "After weeks of fitting herself into one Bolshoi norm or another, Pavlova suddenly bursts out in an adagio with Gordeyev that is a sweeping assertion of her gifts. There is something both casual and electric in her attack that is uniquely Bolshoi, but in the way she spirals and plummets and cuts the air she's unlike any other Russian dancer."

When Pavlova and Gordeyev first appeared in New York in 1973, Deborah Jowitt commented on their "fiercely young out-to-conquer charisma." In 1979, they were still young, fierce and charismatic, and they conquered everyone—the analysts, like Croce, the emoters, like Barnes, and audiences across the board. They became the talk of the town—signing autographs, talking briefly to reporters ("Our lives revolve around the ballet, our art," said Gordeyev) and even appearing in Jack Martin's *New York Post* column as "that hot little pair of Bolshoi superstars" when Jean and Ray Fox threw a party for them. Anna Kisselgoff called them "great dancers" and "the revelation of the season," and John Simon summed up everyone's feelings in a single sentence. Pavlova, like Gordeyev, he wrote, "can make everything stop at the apex of a leap: gravity, time, our heartbeat, mortality itself."

Pavlova and Gordeyev received numerous offers to guest with American companies, and it is to be hoped that they will be allowed to accept them. More than anything else they need nurturing challenges. The blundering Bolshoi repertory threatens to blunt the edges of their style and does nothing to tax their almost infinite resources. As with our hopes for peace, the future of these two dancers must, if they are to survive, include a meeting of East and West.

Spartacus. Photo: G. F. Soloviev

Index

Acknowledgments:
I am most grateful to Mary Clarke and Alastair Macaulay for their advice and assistance. I must also thank the photographers whose work is included in this book for their time and effort, and the Dance Collection at the New York Public Library at Lincoln Center for the use of photographs from the Collection, John Travas for the use of photographs from the London Festival Ballet archive, and Mrs. André Eglevsky for lending pictures from her private collection. Thanks also to Sarah Woodcock for her assistance in finding material from the Theatre Collection of the Victoria and Albert Museum. For their kindness in granting interviews or answering questions, I must thank Sir Anton Dolin, Anthony Dowell, Melissa Hayden, Antoinette Sibley, and Igor Youskevitch, and Suzanne Farrell for suggesting photographs. I thank Universe Books for encouragement and patience, Susan Au for meticulous editing, and most of all, Clovis Ruffin and Dorothy Caeser Chanock for their kindness and their homes, without which this book would yet be unwritten.

Front cover: Peter Martins and Suzanne Farrell in the pas de deux from *Flower Festival in Genzano*. *Photo:* Martha Swope

Back cover: Anna Pavlova and Mikhail Mordkin in *The Autumn Bacchanale*. Cover, *The Play Pictorial*. Victoria and Albert Museum